GUILTY
BY
ASSOCIATION

RUDI
DEKKERS

Copyright © 2011 by Rudi Dekkers

All rights reserved. No part of this book may be used or reproduced in any manner watsoever without written permission, except in the case of brief quotations embodied in article and reviews. For information and permission, please contact the publisher.

Design and layout: Anthony Sclavi and Russell Boldt
Editing: Anna Nething

Printed in the United States of America

ISBN: 978-0-9826687-3-3
Library of Congress Control Number: 2011922026

Published by:
BRIOpress
12 South 6th Street, Suite 1250
Minneapolis, MN 55402

Dedicated
To
Angeline Bianca Chantal

CONTENTS

THANK YOU	1
FOREWORD	3
PROLOGUE	7
FROM GHETTO TO RICHES	21
ONWARD	41
FLYING	51
TO AMERICA AND BACK	65
THE FLYING BUSINESS	75
9/11	91
9/12 PART 1	99
DEAD MAN WALKING	103
9/12 PART 2	121
JOURNALISTS, THE NEWS, AND ME	131
THE TERRORISTS GET THEIR VISAS	161
FALLOUT	179
I SURVIVE	197
MY STORY CONTINUES	209
EPILOGUE	213

THANK YOU

I did hundreds of interviews trying to tell the world the truth about what happened at my flight school after the tragedies of September eleventh. When I read the interviews later in newspapers and on the Internet I was shocked and saddened to see how much information was incorrectly reported. I'm still not sure if this was because of malice or sheer ineptitude, but I decided the only way to get the true story out was to tell it myself. I would have to write a book. My biggest problem? I am not a writer.

I began looking for help. I would need a writer who would listen to me and tell my story my way. I needed someone nearby, someone who knew about flying, and someone who could understand me both in my native Dutch tongue and in English. And I actually found someone who fit the bill: Miriam Jacobs.

Without Miriam, this book would literally not exist. We began our work together with the book proposal. After that, I knew I wanted her to be the writer of my book as well. Miriam and I began our work but this journey was more complicated than we expected.

She taped more than a hundred hours of interviews

with me and then wrote the book in English. Using this draft, a publisher in the Netherlands added some material and translated it all back into Dutch. In September of 2008 they released *De Vliegende Hollander*, which made the bestseller list in the Netherlands. With this English version we are ready to bring it to a world audience. Through it all, from Dutch to English to Dutch and then back to English again, Miriam has stayed true to my story.

Friends of mine who read her manuscript say that it sounds like me, as if I am sitting with them at the kitchen table telling them my story. Of all the successes of this book, this is the one I am most grateful for. Thank you, Miriam, for bringing my voice out.

Rudi Dekkers

FOREWORD

I heard Rudi Dekkers before I saw him. He was standing out of my line of sight in a chaotic room full of U.S. government agents at his tiny flight school in Venice, Florida, fighting for my right to be there.

The events of September 11, 2001 are etched on our nation's collective memory. For me, that day and time is inextricably connected with Rudi.

I was working as a television reporter at the NBC affiliate in southwest Florida. As I was driving to work one September morning, I heard that a plane had slammed into the World Trade Center. In a matter of minutes, my photographer and I were trying to connect with former U.S. Intelligence officers who had retired in our sleepy community. The question was simple: Who wanted to hurt us, and why?

A day later the answers were much clearer, thanks in part to Rudi Dekkers.

My pager woke up before I did on September twelfth. A newsroom manager told me that government agents were at a private home in Venice. No one knew why. My photographer was part of the crowd there, watching and waiting.

It was instantly clear to me. The terrorist connection had to be a flight school. I lived close to a flight school in my hometown on Florida's east coast. I was accustomed to seeing young, Middle Eastern men who had come to town to learn how to fly. Venice, Florida is a well-known retirement mecca. It had a small, general aviation airport that I figured could be the only attraction for foreign-born terrorists.

I picked up my photographer near the house in Venice. Neither of us had ever been to the airport. As we approached the property, the first building we saw was Huffman Aviation. The parking lot was swarming with dark SUVs and men wheeling out file cabinets. We slipped inside with the camera rolling. This story nearly ended there. We were spotted by government agents, and our ejection was in motion.

That's when I heard Rudi Dekkers. He boldly and loudly declared that it was his building and we could stay. We continued shooting as Rudi argued, making the most of our reprieve. As the ruckus continued, we were swept into a small break room. A few minutes later Rudi joined us. He slipped me a piece of paper. It was a photocopy of two driver's licenses: one issued to Mohammed Atta, the other to Marwan al-Shehhi.

Those names, that once seemed so strange, are now familiar. When the agents left, Rudi laid out his story. He showed us the planes the future hijackers flew, explained in great detail the certifications the two men earned during their time at Huffman, and told us where they came from and where they went. Rudi described his interactions with both Atta and Shehhi and how they related to each other and their fellow flight students. Our interview nearly filled a sixty-minute satellite window. Within a few hours, it was fed to the world.

In the years since the terror attacks, nothing that Rudi Dekkers shared that morning has been discredited. His account profoundly enhanced our understanding of who these men were and how they moved among us.

Huffman Aviation is most closely associated with the 9/11 terrorists, but it was not the only flight school that unwittingly trained hijackers. Rudi Dekkers stands out because he was willing to stick his neck out, he told his story over and over again, and the insights he shared provided a timely and accurate account to a nation starving for information.

The willingness to speak his mind is a hallmark of Rudi's character. Six months after the terror attacks, he made news again. This time, he revealed to me that the U.S. government had issued visa extensions to the two deceased hijackers. The information rekindled a storm of criticism against government agencies. As a direct result, the INS was dismantled and ultimately the Department of Homeland Security was born.

My interactions with Rudi were undoubtedly fruitful. Building a trusting relationship with Rudi and learning what he knew and experienced contributed to my winning an Edward R. Murrow award. More importantly, his recollections served a public purpose. Rudi's accounts are part of the official record as compiled by the 9/11 Commission report. However, it stops far short of telling his entire story.

A Dutch citizen with a controversial past, Rudi made himself a target by standing up and delivering in a time of crisis. It was a costly decision. His business crumbled and his marriage did, too. At the same time, he was testifying in front of Congress and being hounded by Immigration. He could have avoided much of it if he kept his head down and his mouth shut. But that's not Rudi Dekkers' style.

Amy Oshier

PROLOGUE

The weather outside is nasty when I get out of bed, which is the exception rather than the rule in Naples, Florida. When I saw Barefoot Beach for the first time it was love at first sight. The sandy beach is pristine, the sky is a perfect blue 350 days of the year, the temperature rarely dips below forty degrees Fahrenheit, and the breathtaking sunsets over the Gulf of Mexico are framed by palm trees. The whole scene looks like a vacation postcard. However, on this day at the end of January 2003, it is an inexplicably chilly twenty degrees.

My morning ritual is always short and functional, but today I won't even take time for breakfast. Because it is so ridiculously cold—it'll end up being one of the coldest days in the modern history of Florida—I do not automatically put on my usual summer garb, which lies next to my bed. Instead, I grab a pair of long pants, pull a vest on over my long sleeve shirt, and grab my big leather jacket, which I rarely get to wear here. I silently wish my still-sleeping wife a pleasant day and I walk down the stairs. I need to leave immediately—it's six a.m.

With my remote, I open my garage door, start my bright red Viper, and drive into the cold. The streets are empty at this early hour, but even in rush hour, my sports car does not stand out. Naples is a city where the rich and famous have come to build their mansions and to moor their luxury yachts. Many of the residents are retired sports and movie stars, cashed-out investment bankers, golf-loving ex-CEOs, and has-been political honchos.

Driving between the huge estates and gated communities, I soon get to Interstate 75 and drive north through the dawn. As soon as I can, I go over the maximum speed limit, because no matter how much fun driving this car is, the bumper stickers are right: "I'd rather be flying." The trip from my house to Fort Meyers International Airport, known by its call letters RSW, takes only eighteen minutes. I wonder if the orange groves are going to be harmed by this unusual cold as I take the turn on 131. From this turnoff, it is only six more minutes to the private facility of this airport, the area used exclusively by people who own their own airplanes. The moment I arrive, I run from my car to seek shelter inside, away from the biting wind.

Once inside, I grab a cup of coffee and add lots of milk to make it palatable. I don't really like American coffee, but over the last few years, I have reluctantly made the change from hot tea to the coffee Americans seem to prefer. After I check in at the front desk, I hold the cup in both my hands, and the warmth makes my hands tingle. Tony Douangdara is also there and has just finished his morning cup. He is a great guy in his late thirties and an excellent helicopter pilot. He and his beautiful Hughes MD 500 helicopter are for hire as an air taxi. He recently started working for NBC television, ferrying guests to the various studios and bringing camera people to news sites and journalists to press conferences.

"Hi Rudi! I bet you're going to Venice," he says by way of greeting. Rudi is my name now that I live in the US, but I am still 'Ruud' to my Dutch friends.

"Of course," I say. Everybody here, and probably just about everybody in the United States, knows that I am the owner of Huffman Aviation, a flight school in Venice, Florida. The flight school and I have been in the news for about a year and a half. We have both become famous and infamous—it has been bad for business.

"I'm also going in that direction," says Tony, as he zips up his jacket and gets ready to walk out of the hangar. "Maybe we'll see each other there."

"I'll call you when I'm in the air," I say.

Tony calmly walks into the cold on his way to a group of helicopters and private airplanes waiting for their pilots. A chill runs down my back, but I don't think it is because of the cold. It feels more like a sort of envy. Even though Tony earns less than the average cop, he does get to fly a helicopter every day, and it is possible that my flying days are done.

I take a quick leak and drink another cup of coffee, mainly to postpone going out. All these years in a warm climate have thinned my sturdy Dutch blood and I find the cold hard to take. I casually tell the person behind the counter that I will see him later, and walk to the door of the hangar. I hesitate a moment when I feel the chill. One of the ground crew guys notices and walks toward me. Wearing his thick winter jacket, he has just finished filling the gas tanks of a few planes. He offers me a ride in his golf cart, which will bring me to my Hiller HF 1100 helicopter. Under ordinary circumstances, I wouldn't consider taking the offer, as it's ridiculous to avoid walking a few hundred feet, but today I gratefully accept.

The Hiller is wet from last night's rain, and some of the water on the rotors is frozen. The moment I open the cabin door and step in, condensation hits the glass and fogs up. I curse loudly in my native Dutch. I know it doesn't help, but for reasons I can't explain, it makes me feel better. I get out of the helicopter again with a large cloth to wipe the blades dry. I do the rest of my pre-flight check quickly but thoroughly. I know how important this is from bitter experience. I have lost too many friends in accidents, most of which could have been prevented if they had only taken the time to methodically check off every item on their pre-flight checklist. I will always remember Kevin, a racecar driver and playboy from Naples. His idea of a pre-flight check was a brisk walk around the airplane. I don't know how many times I called him on that, and even though I must have sounded like an overbearing mother hen, I would admonish him, "Kevin, you have to be more careful, you're playing with your life." He would just laugh and nod and ignore my advice. He disregarded my advice on the last day I saw him. He had told me just before his flight that everything was going really well in his life and he was looking forward to taking a little pleasure trip with some friends. He did not rent an airplane from me that day, and he cut his pre-flight check short. A few hours later, he and his friends were dead.

As much as I love flying, I never take any of it for granted. I notice every sound, every vibration, every unusual sign, no matter how minor they might seem. All I can say is, after more than a quarter-century of flying, I am still alive. I tell all my pilots they have to do a careful pre-flight check, concentrate as they are flying, and keep their skills up to par through regular checks by an instructor. I am known to be fanatical about safety and I think that is a good thing.

I remove the covers, which keep the blades from turning in the wind, by loosening their bungee cords. I rotate the blades a quarter turn to make sure nothing is obstructing them. After the big blades, I inspect the small tail rotor. I turn this one as well and check for any give. When everything looks all right, I walk to the side and look at the engine and main-gear box oil levels. After that, I check the gas tank. I make a mental note: about 18 gallons. I open the fuel panel and make sure everything looks all right, and it does. But I'm wrong. Everything is not all right.

I close the fuel panel, and I finally climb into the cabin. I leave the door open for a short while to let some of the moisture evaporate as I dry off the inside of the window. I check the fuel gauge inside the cabin, which confirms what I already know: I have 18.2 gallons of fuel. Since I bought 14 gallons yesterday, I know I have enough fuel to make this short trip. This helicopter uses about 15 gallons per hour. When you are flying VF (visual flight rules, meaning that you have clear and full vision), you must always give yourself a half hour of reserve. Including that reserve, I have enough fuel for about forty-five minutes. My flight from Ft. Myers, Florida, to Venice is only about twenty minutes, and I plan to re-fuel at the pump at my own flight school there. I can sell gas to myself at a cheaper rate than I would pay as a retail customer at Ft. Myers.

I start the motor to let it warm up slowly on this cold day. I check the collective to make sure it is in the correct position. The collective determines the position of the rotating blades and gives the helicopter its upward pull. Then I check the cyclic (the joystick between your legs). After I complete these routine checks, I let her warm up for about a minute more. During that time, I get out of the helicopter one more time. The pilot operating handbook does not consider this last check absolutely necessary, but because I like to be sure, I always do one extra visual check to make sure that the motor seems to be turning without any problems. Everything looks, sounds, and feels reassuringly ordinary, just the way I like it. Good—it's time to go!

I try to buckle my shoulder and hip straps—the aviation equivalent of getting strapped into an infant car seat—but I need to adjust the shoulder straps, which do not fit over my bulky leather jacket. As soon as I am comfortable, I increase the gas. The helicopter hovers gently over the ground, about two feet over the spot where she had been sitting. I call up the tower and ask permission to fly against the wind, which is blowing from the east, in the direction of Venice.

Tony left about ten minutes ahead of me, heading northwest. After the tower OKs my request, I pull on the collective, and the helicopter lifts vertically off the ground. As I am rising, I call Tony and tell him that I want to talk to him later on, but first I have to pass the next airport in my path, Page Field Airport. I usually pass the airspace of Page Field on the east side; although I am not required to inform them of my presence, I do it out of politeness.

"Helicopter at FH 543, good morning, request to pass through your airspace."

Permission is granted immediately—the tower isn't busy at this early hour. A moment later, Tony announces that he is leaving the Page Field airspace. I make an automatic mental note that he is about twenty miles further than I am. As much as I detest the cold, the helicopter's motor loves this weather and is running better than ever. Instead of the usual 115 knots, she is humming along at 130 knots.

From where I am, I can see the exquisite Gulf of Mexico. It is a beautiful flight over many islands and inlets. The beaches are flat with almost blindingly white sand. However, the most beautiful sights of all are the sea animals frolicking about. I see dolphins, sharks, and huge schools of fish shimmering in the water.

I fly over the group of square buildings that together form Lee Memorial Hospital. Right before me is the mouth of the Caloosahatchee River. This seventy-five mile long river begins at Lake Okeechobee to the east. Here at the mouth, right before it pours out into in the Gulf of Mexico, it is almost three miles wide. Although I do not enjoy flying over long stretches of water, I have no choice in the matter, since Venice lies on the other side. The helicopter is flying smoothly, so there is no real reason for me to worry. I bought it secondhand three years ago for $90,000. Together with Bob Martin, the head mechanic from my repair shop in Venice, I have put in almost $70,000 worth of repairs and renovations. I fly almost daily and I make sure it is well-maintained. Of course there is nothing to worry about. I breathe out and relax.

After flying about a hundred feet over the river, I find out that my confidence is misplaced. I suddenly realize that my motor has less power. The blades start spinning more slowly and at the moment that I fully realize this, I have already lost thirty percent of my power. Then I hear a funny stuttering sound. If your engine stops, the small rotor in the back will not keep you flying straight anymore. The whole helicopter will move to the left; to prevent that you correct the rotation with a push on the foot pedal. A lot of training goes into making these maneuvers automatic reactions, but in doing them, I lose another precious second. It is only then I realize that I am losing altitude as well as power. I look at my gas gauge and see that I am on empty. I know that can't be true after a mere ten minutes of flying, but I have no time to consider how that could have happened.

In one cool, rational moment, I realize I might not make it, and it gives me some small comfort to think I might die in my beloved helicopter. I know that I started flying over the river at about 500 feet and by now, I have already lost a precious 200 feet. For a moment, I think that the wind can blow me back to the land. I make a sharp left turn and immediately see that it is a wasted effort, but at least I will have less of a distance to swim to shore. At the same time, for reasons I cannot explain, I undo the bottom buckle of my safety belt and open the door to my right. The third simultaneous action I perform is to call Tony.

"Tony, I'm going down. I'm going to crash into the river, right by the hospital."

"Are you kidding me?" I hear his voice say.

"No, I'm going down. Gotta go."

I switch immediately to the radio frequency of the tower of Ft. Myers. I report my emergency to them as well, and then I focus completely on flying my helicopter. My speed is diminished to about 60 knots without the power of my motor, but with a strong wind at my back I must still be moving at about 85 knots. I can see from my instruments that I am also sinking like a rock at about 800 feet per minute.

I know what is going to happen and I know I have only a few seconds left. The statistics are grim: eighty percent of all helicopter pilots who crash in the water do not survive. But I have never been average and I do not give up hope. In addition, I have had some unusual training in how to get myself out of tight spots—I was well prepared for this specific stituation.

A few years ago, I had a British pupil named John at one of my flight schools. He was already an accomplished pilot who just needed to get his American pilot's license. He noticed my Gazelle helicopter and asked me if I was the owner. I told him that it was indeed my proud possession. He then told me that he had been a flight instructor in the British Army, which used Gazelles for reconnaissance work. It didn't take me long to offer him free flying lessons in return for his private instruction in advanced flying methods in the Gazelle. John let me do things that normal helicopter pilots never get to try.

One of John's lessons was supposed to be a theoretical one: his instructions on how to land on water and survive. The standard American instruction is to turn the helicopter onto its side. The theory is that the water will slow down the blades and then you can safely exit once you are in the water. Great theory, but it doesn't work in real life, John explained—hence the huge fatality rate. The problem is that the blades break off the moment they hit the water and then slice through the cabin before it is safely encased in water, which usually has deadly results. He told me that you have to land the helicopter flat into the water as if you were landing on level ground. The moment the helicopter hits the water, it will sink, and the water will then protect you against the spinning blades even if they break off. Because the blades are the heaviest part of the helicopter, the entire structure will then tilt to the side. Once you are underwater, you can exit from the door, which will be pointing toward the surface of the water. That was the theory and it made a lot of sense.

I use the auto rotation, which means that I adjust the collective so that the blades are turned in the non-lift position. Because of the downward momentum, the blades will then passively spin due to the air, which is now pushing from below. Just before I hit the water's surface, I move the lever and make the blades change their position. I now have a bit of uplift, somewhat softening the blow of the landing. I emphasize—somewhat.

prologue

I have not been able to slow the forward motion. I calculate later that the jolt I get is equivalent to hitting a concrete wall at eighty miles an hour. I know instinctively what is going to happen: the huge front window of the helicopter will break and the entire helicopter will function like a huge scoop, taking in water before sinking to the bottom. Is it possible that my instinctive act of loosening my bottom buckle was to allow me to take in one last huge breath? My last act in the airborne helicopter is to take in the biggest breath of my life.

My training is good enough to help me stay rational. But at the moment of impact, I am no more than a rag doll, and all that air I inhaled is immediately knocked out of my lungs. I can feel the impact all the way down my spine, and in seconds I am hanging upside down in a helicopter that is sinking to the bottom of the river. I reflexively breathe in and fill my lungs with ice-cold water. Half a second later, the helicopter turns, lying with the right side down at an angle.

For a moment, I panic. Everything has gone wrong and the game is over. I am freezing, and I despair. I am hanging upside down in my shoulder harness and can't see more than two feet ahead of me. I am stuck and even if I could free myself, I am still a dead man. The opening in front of me looks like a modern sculpture of Plexiglas splinters so I dare not swim through it. I'm afraid that if I try to find the left door, I will get disoriented in the cabin. The right door, which I unlocked while flying, is underneath me. The door has opened a few inches, but the bottom of the river blocks it from opening further.

The panic only lasts an instant and then my rational mind is back in charge. The voice of reason says, "Rudi, Rudi, Rudi, if you panic, you will definitely not survive this. You have ten seconds at the most. You have to be calm right now and think about what you're going to do."

With my lungs full of water, I cannot breathe, but once the panic leaves me, I don't seem to need air. I am suddenly peaceful and content as if I have enough air for the rest of my life. Actually, I just might be right in that assessment. With my foot, I search around for a toehold. I find the crack in the door to my right and feel the sand at the bottom of the river. Unfortunately, I am still hanging in my shoulder harness and can't get out. Not only is my slightly overweight body working against me in my upside-down position, but my jacket is wet and the wet leather is glued to the shoulder belt. I see this and soberly note that this is not a good situation.

I don't see any white light and my life does not flash in front of me. I stay rational and sharp and think at an amazing speed. One thought is definitely, "This is the end of Rudi Dekkers." I have never been the kind of person who spends a lot of time thinking about the past and this moment at the bottom of the river is no different. I think about the future, about what will happen after my death. I think about my wife Astrid and about my children, who are my greatest responsibility and the greatest joy in my life. My children, my three beautiful girls, are old enough and strong enough to do without their dad. I know they'll be all right.

I take comfort in the fact that I have a huge amount of life insurance. The insurance should pay out about five million dollars, resolving all my debts in one fell swoop. For Astrid, there will be about a million left over, enough to live on for quite a while. For her, it might even be a relief. She wanted to get rid of me, and she will be pleasantly surprised by how much money she will get. She commented recently, her voice dripping with sarcasm, "Your empire has pretty much collapsed by now." She is right, of course. Ambassador Airways, my first flight school, emptied out about two months after 9/11. My power to run Florida Air, the airline I had started, has been taken away from me, while Huffman Aviation, the most beautiful company I have ever owned, can no longer keep its head above water. I have fought like a maniac for a year and a half, but it cannot be done. The bank has called in my loans; this afternoon I have a meeting to sign the papers that will sell Huffman. It doesn't look like that is going to happen now.

Two years ago I was living the good life. All my projects were running well. I was responsible for graduating about 200 licensed pilots a year and I was on my way to becoming the CEO of a new airline in Florida. On paper, I was worth twelve million dollars. Huffman Air, all that was left of the empire I had built with such great effort, I had intended to sell that afternoon, and I'd be left with a grand total of $57,676.

When I asked Astrid, for the first and only time in our twenty-year marriage, to take a job to help our family through these difficult financial times, she refused. I couldn't understand it because she had never been disloyal and she had seen how much I had suffered the last few years, but she left me in the lurch. I realize suddenly, at the bottom of this river, that she has proven how well she has adapted to the US way of life. She is planning to start divorce proceedings and I am sure she will demand the children as well as the house. So what is left for me? My helicopter is gone, my reputation has been damaged beyond repair, my material goods are gone, and my family is about to be torn apart. I figure I might as well just sit here and accept what is coming next. It can't be all that bad.

FROM GHETTO TO RICHES

I remember nothing of my first six years. I know I lived with my parents in Apeldoorn, about ninety kilometers or fifty-five miles east of Amsterdam, but everything else that I know from that time comes from the stories my parents told me later on. I might have spent time playing innocent childhood games during those years, but by the time my parents moved to Amsterdam in 1962, that childhood joy was gone.

Most Americans know Amsterdam either as a haven for legal drug use and prostitution or as an art mecca where they can browse museums and see the works of famous Dutch painters such as Rembrandt and Van Gogh. Tourists love the picturesque houses built beside the canals, and they amuse themselves by taking guided tours in the glass-enclosed barges.

For me, growing up in Amsterdam, the canal was where our houseboat floated and my neighborhood was the old Jewish ghetto. Though the "Jordaan" had been Amsterdam's famous Jewish quarter before WWII, the Nazi occupation radically changed the area after astounding numbers of Jews living there were rounded up and taken off to concentration camps.

When I lived there it was just a poor, tough, bitter neighborhood.

My mother, father, and I lived on a houseboat, in a canal next to the Lijnbaansgracht, a street that intersected with the Palmgracht Street. My father bought old barges and turned them into houseboats. Ours was called the "Madretsmaduo," which is Dutch for "Old Amsterdam" spelled backwards. The boat still exists; I last saw it when I visited Amsterdam in 2008.

It might have been a picturesque houseboat, but living there was not enjoyable. It was cold and reeked of poverty. My parents were unable to provide a dependable income and I can remember nights when I woke up from the rumbling of my empty stomach. There was always lots of work to do and only meager bits of material comfort. We did not have electricity or running water—our faucet was the public hand pump across the street. With water at a premium and only the most primitive washing facilities, personal hygiene was minimal. The one time we did have electricity was when my father bought an old car, which he parked opposite the boat and rigged so that the boat had power, but this huge luxury did not last long.

In those days, clothes were not washed every day, but only once a week, and that was true for both my classmates and me. This would not have been a terrible problem, except that I was a bed wetter. To my shame, I was still unable to control my bladder at night until the age of ten, and I often had to go to school in the clothes I slept in. No wonder they nicknamed me "stinky animal." My experiences with the taunting scum, who had no pity on me in those days, have resulted in my adult habit of showering twice or three times per day, a habit undoubtedly connected to those miserable days of my youth.

It is also quite clear to me now, as I have raised children of my own and understand a bit about their psychology, why I was still a bed wetter at that late age. My bed wetting must have originated in the fear that I lived with, growing up in such an unsafe environment. Walking on the streets would often result in a fistfight and the situation at home was hardly any better. Your parents ought to protect you from the scary world and your home should be safe territory, but my parents lacked the psychological insight and self-discipline to protect me. In almost all ways they were opposites. He was authoritarian and brusque while she was much too emotional. She was too young and inexperienced; he was too old and hardened.

My mother Zwaantje drank and cried a lot and had no idea how to run a family or a house. Even if she had known how to run a house, my mother lacked the equipment with which to do it, and our houseboat was a mess. The other smell that I associate with my poverty is cigarettes. Both my parents smoked, and even then, I thought it was a disgusting habit. Before my tenth birthday I swore I would never drink and never smoke and have kept that promise, with the exception of an annual gulp of champagne to celebrate the New Year.

When I was born, my father was twice as old as my mother. Athough I didn't know it at the time, he already had several children from other relationships. Once I was added into that mix, we formed what is now known as a classic dysfunctional family.

My father had a short fuse, but he was smart, handy, and very clever. If his eyes saw something, his hands could make it. He had an HTS diploma (high level technical school), which was quite an accomplishment; because of his degree, he never had a problem finding work. However, his contrary character ensured that all these jobs were short-lived. He could get away with his erratic behavior at home, but his employers, of course, would not accept it. My father messed things up for himself everywhere by saying the wrong things, by rubbing people the wrong way, and by seeking out conflict. The result was that he was regularly out of work. When that happened, my mother would go back to work for a while as a waitress in the Hotel de Pool, situated opposite Beurs van Berlage, the stock market in Amsterdam. I would frequently find myself at the other side of that short fuse—occasionally he would beat me so hard I would pass out.

Though he was frequently out of work, my father was not lazy. He could always find something to do. For instance, he would find discarded furniture on the streets, bring it home, restore it, and sell it again. He had no shortage of creativity and inventiveness and a good sense of what people would like; since what he made was well-constructed and useful, he could always sell his wares. To supplement this irregular source of income, my mother occasionally arranged for him to work as a concierge at the Hotel de Pool.

I only remember my father having one success story. It is the one time that his contrariness, persistence, and technical knowledge created a positive result. Somehow, my father became obsessed with the idea of becoming an amateur radio operator, or ham operator. With found materials, he built his own radio in our houseboat. It was painstaking work, requiring every ounce of his minimal patience. I had always been in awe of his big strong hands, but my respect increased when I saw him working with all those small parts. When he eventually managed to get some noise out of his own radio, I was amazed. This was a whole lot more impressive than reupholstering an old chair. From then on, my father spent a lot of time with his homemade radio. With childlike innocence and enthusiasm, he told me from which far-off places he was receiving his signals. This was before TV and mobile phones and it was a revelation—a whole new world opened up for us. After a while, it began to bother him that this innocent and fascinating hobby was actually illegal, as broadcasting on the frequency of 27 MHz was forbidden by law.

I can now see that my entrepreneurial bent and love of finding an innovative way to make things happen probably came from my father. He showed these characteristics in good form by transforming his irritation into a strategy to make his radio hobby legal for himself and others. He figured that the way to change the law would be to create a useful and helpful function for the amateur radio operators. To that end, he created an organization called "Edelweiss," which was going to help stranded motorists. The ANWB was then and still is the Dutch equivalent of AAA in the United States, providing emergency roadside service for its members. In those days, there were fewer garages, and cell phones were nonexistent, so that fast, effective communication was not necessarily available to a stranded motorist. Even an organization willing to help motorists in need was therefore not always able to provide prompt and efficient service. He suggested that Edelweiss could solve this problem. The idea was simple and effective: in order to be able to help drivers, you need cheap and easy-to-operate transmitters and a legal frequency. Edelweiss just happened to have them. The strategy was a success, and the law was changed in part because of my father's support and effort. The Dutch national organization of radio amateurs, called De Vereneging Radio Zend Amateurs, later acknowledged my father for his groundbreaking work.

Because of the physical and emotional stress at home, I realized at an early age that I would have to protect myself against the world. I realized that the best defense was not only to keep the outer world away from me, but also to make sure that my own emotions would not get the better of me. When I saw my mother's unbridled emotional outbursts I did not understand how she could live like that. It wasn't that I didn't have that kind of raw emotion, but I was absolutely determined not to live my life with so little control. I made a firm determination to keep my feelings to myself and never reveal them to anybody. Long before I knew how to put the idea into words, I resolved to make my decisions based on rational thinking.

From the windows of our houseboat, you could see the Palmgracht Street; my view of the world was not much bigger than that. My school was on the same street and on the very rare occasions that I played outside, it was, again, on the Palmgracht. My father thought that playing outside was a waste of time. If he saw me outside, he would call me inside and put me to work with endless chores. When I was nine years old, somebody commissioned him to build a houseboat—of course, he required my help with that project. What was particularly galling to me was that this was the year my classmates would occasionally ask me to play outside. It wasn't out of the goodness of their hearts—it happened that they were one man short in their soccer team, so I was useful to them. Because I lacked experience, I would never have been asked under ordinary circumstances, so I felt excited and honored to be included. Occasionally, I would slip away and go to the playground, where I might get in a precious half-hour to play before my mother would call me home. I knew I shouldn't have taken that half-hour, but the temptation was too big.

If, by chance, my father did not need me for an hour or so, I would go to the Dam Square, the main public square in Amsterdam with some homemade supplies to shine shoes. I was quick and handy and had an instinctive ability to find clients. In some mysterious way, I found a way to combine some of my mother's charm with a little of my father's cleverness; by the time I was eleven years old, I had developed a lucrative shoeshine business.

I think that it was my romantic imagination that made me believe that playing outside with the boys would be fun. The reality is that big city life often breeds aggression. Everybody in my neighborhood found their way into a gang, and these gangs endlessly battled with each other in fistfights on the street. The rules in my neighborhood were no different from those of tough, gritty neighborhoods all over the world: Your membership in a gang put you at risk of being beaten up by the rival gang, but at least the members of your own gang would be obliged to protect you—at a minimum, they would probably avenge you. Because I was never allowed to play on the streets, I never had a chance to join any gang, which meant that I had to walk the streets without any protection. My walk home from school often resulted in a beating and I frequently came home with a black eye or a bleeding lip.

One of the few luxuries my shoeshine business allowed me was taking in a Sunday matinee at a small cinema. Unfortunately, I often had to pay a steep price for that pleasure, too, since the neighborhood bullies were usually waiting for me at the end of the performance to beat me up. I was elated when I found the back door of that cinema, and for a few weeks I was able to run home in safety. That was, of course, until they, too, discovered the back door.

Westerns were a favorite offering in that small cinema; they became my favorites, too. On those Sunday afternoons, I met the legendary American cowboys, the good guys who beat the legendary American bad boys, namely the Indians. I saw these rough and heroic men galloping wildly on horseback over boundless prairies, loving freedom and justice, surrounded by breathtaking natural beauty. Even though much of the movie was taken up with fistfights and shooting, from the safety and comfort of my seat, it was wonderful to lose myself in that heroic dream world. Not until the end credits would roll up did I realize that I had my own Wild West adventure right outside that door.

Elementary school was hell, and to make things worse, I was not a brilliant student. I was fidgety; I lacked the ability to concentrate for long and had too much energy to spend much time on any one subject. I simply couldn't sit still. Actually, I still can't; I always need something to do. My inability to focus resulted in terrible marks and I had to repeat a grade twice. My parents were so frustrated with my lack of academic performance that they considered placing me in a "special" school. To my horror, all those "special" students looked like they were retarded and I was horrified to think I might be put in that environment. I knew that I was easily distracted, but it had never occurred to me that I might be seen as retarded.

Mrs. Van Eck, my teacher at the time, was the only one who had a different opinion. One day, she called my parents and told them that she thought I could be doing better. She asked my parents for their permission to observe me to try to figure out what was actually happening. In her eyes, I must have been an unusual child, a loner, but I doubt that my parents had any inkling as to what she was saying. All they knew was that I got bad grades, so they agreed to the experiment.

Thank God for that because my teacher's instincts proved to be right. I wasn't retarded; on the contrary, I was very intelligent and just needed some coaching. That, in itself, was a comforting piece of news, but the next part was even better. Ms. Van Eck decided to look out for me for a while. She mentored me and provided the direction I was lacking at home. Because of her help, it took me only six months to make up for the two years I had lost. I did not turn out to be an overnight genius, and my grades remained average C-, but things went a lot better for me once she appeared in my life. The one thing I excelled at was doing math in my head—a skill that later came in handy, but the most direct result was that I could go on to high school at the Marnixschool.

I also found a solution to having the crap beaten out of me. When I was twelve, my father sent me to judo classes. It was an excellent decision, which delivered unexpectedly quick results. To my own surprise, I soon realized that I was much stronger than most guys my age. The self-confidence that came with that knowledge was perhaps just as important as my self-defense techniques. Whatever the reason, the bullies now left me alone.

When I was fourteen, there were five of us living our dreary existence on our houseboat. Despite all their quibbling, my parents had conceived my sister Yvonne (1963) and my brother Marcel (1965), so the houseboat was now a lot more crowded.

Then, in just one moment, everything changed. My father's grandmother died, and my father inherited her house. It was a huge house that my grandfather had built himself in 1932 in Bennekom, eighty kilometers or fifty miles southeast of Amsterdam. Once we moved there, things improved immediately. We moved from the busy, violent city to the deep peace and rest of the country, from that horrible cold, miserable boat to a comfortable, cozy villa.

Instead of living in an urban setting with screaming poverty and violence, we were suddenly surrounded by verdant woods with lots of animal life; a whole new world opened up to me. I saw animals that I had never seen outside of picture books, right outside our house, running up trees and flying in the air. I petted docile cows in the meadow, and I went to every riding school I could find to try and ride horses, just like my heroes in the western movies. I got a new bicycle that meant complete freedom and mobility. I loved our new life; I had the powerful realization that this huge improvement was the result of the decision to move just fifty miles away. It was a lesson I would always remember.

Rural living was even good for my grades in school. I also had some instant social status and clout, since the farm boys saw me as a sophisticated city guy. I excelled in school now, so I was moved to college-prep classes. Together with my new best friend, Martin van Dinteren, I cycled every day to the nearby city of Wageningen because the local high school did not offer courses that were challenging enough. I loved history and algebra, but most of all, I remember that I loved the girls. In my sweet memory, the entire place was overrun with pretty girls!

However, most classroom subjects still interested me less than all the exciting things I could see outside my school window. I spent my hours after class exploring my surroundings. I became convinced that I could learn anything I set my mind to, at least anything that really interested me.

I was a changed person and easily left my Amsterdam persona behind. My parents were busy with my brother and sister and I loved my new freedom. I spent time with my new friends, did odd jobs, and every chance I got I went to Manege Selterskamp, a riding school owned by Mr. Ketler. In exchange for working in the barns, I was allowed to take some horseback-riding lessons, and I loved it. Those big, powerful animals were calming and inspiring at the same time and I felt completely at ease with them. I talked to the sweet horses while I was brushing them and sweeping their stalls. I spent so much time there that after a while it felt more like home than my own home. My grades plummeted, and instead of being on track for the University, I was thrown back with the shop kids in the simplest academic classes. But I became a good enough rider that I started teaching others how to ride, which was my ideal situation: doing what I loved and getting paid for it. What a great combination!

But my first real money was earned by pumping gas for Mr. Kokee when I was fifteen. It was easy work with good pay and I had no problem working Saturdays and many afternoons. I earned a surprisingly large amount of money, including many tips. My mistake was in bragging about it to my father.

My mother had quickly found work in our new town; after all, she was an experienced waitress and good at her job. At this point, she was earning the major portion of our family income, but I think she worked not just because we needed the money, but also because it put some distance between her and my father for a few hours. My father remained exactly who he had always been: a man with a bad attitude. In our small community, that quickly became more obvious than it had been in the big city. It didn't seem to bother him that he was socially isolated or that his meager earnings kept us around the poverty level.

I should have realized all this before I told him with great pride how much Mr. Kokee was paying me. My father, who was by now in his mid-fifties, was jealous, and he lashed out at me. He immediately decided that I should pay for my keep, which would require turning over three quarters of my income. I was in tears at this injustice, and I thought his demand was ridiculous, so I simply refused. My father was not used to having anybody oppose his will and we had a huge fight. He would not give in and neither would I. The longer we argued the worse it got. In the end, he threw me out of the house. He told me that if I was not willing to pay for my keep, I had no right to be there.

Seething with rage, I took off without thinking on my bicycle, riding automatically to the stables. Once I got there, I asked Mr. Ketler if I could rent a room, and moved in that same night. The money I earned pumping gas had given me an enormous feeling of freedom. I was fifteen years old and I had emancipated myself, even though I was now living in a miserable little room in a cold stable. But I was now sure about one thing: I was the only one who made decisions about my own life.

One of my first decisions was not to go to school for a while. School was just a waste of time that kept me from much more pleasant activities such as friends, horses, and earning money. I thought that since this was a rational decision, that meant it was right. I had enough proof to show me that emotional decisions, such as showing your pride in your earnings, always worked out wrong, but rational ones did not. Being a truant suited my style and after a while, I decided to drop out of school all together. A horseback rider does not need a high school diploma—no horse will ask you for one.

I was truly happy and horseback riding was the only thing that mattered. If I was not riding, I cleaned out stalls or gave classes. Though my friends Martin van Dinteren and Eddie Hulshof were still going to school, I saw a lot of them. That idyllic existence lasted about a year-and-a-half, until I realized it would eventually be a dead-end life. If I didn't want to shovel manure or clean up for other people for the rest of my life, I knew I needed a high school diploma.

It took a while before I could swallow my pride. I hadn't seen my father in months, though I had visited my mother and my younger brother and sister regularly behind his back. I rode home on my bicycle and told my father that I had decided to finish school. Was it okay if I came back home? In this confrontation our roles were reversed. This time, I took the initiative and came up with a proposal, and it was almost impossible for him to refuse me. I have to think that he respected me for taking my life into my own hands. He agreed, but he had no intention of making it easy for me. He would not give me back my old room, which he had given to my younger sister, so from then on, I had to sleep in the hallway. I knew intuitively that my punishment resulted from his feeling of impotence. He could not refuse me shelter, but he could choose to make my life miserable. He still insisted that I would have to look after myself and pay for my own schoolbooks. He even demanded three-quarters of my earnings. I was astonished that after all these months of estrangement he would still behave like such a jerk, but I was determined to reach my goal. I decided to make a wise choice for myself. I could not go to school full-time while living at the stables, so I tried to view my last year of high school as an investment that was worth moving back home for. Of course, I lied to my father about my earnings from then on.

For my sixteenth birthday, my parents gave me a Kreidler motorcycle. Though the gift was meant as a reconciliation present, it left a bitter taste in my mouth, since I had earned a good deal of the money for it myself. Years later, my father was still bragging about the expensive present he'd given me for that birthday.

He also gave me another present. He had decided it was time for me to become a man so he took me to the red-light district in Arnhem, which was roughly forty kilometers, or twenty-five miles south of us. I was horribly nervous. I had wandered through the red-light district a few times, but the idea that you could go inside and sample the wares had never even occurred to me. And now I was going to be forced to. He stopped in front of a door and when it opened, he asked how much it cost.

A woman's voice answered, "Twenty-five guilders."

He paid the woman, pushed me inside, and said, "All right Rudi, she will make a man out of you."

Once I was inside and the curtain closed, I told the woman that she could keep the money; I didn't want to do anything. We talked for about fifteen minutes and then I walked out. My father never said a thing or asked me any questions about it.

Then my life became even more confusing. I was back in school, trying to get my high school diploma, and suddenly my parents decided to emigrate. We had been in Bennekom for less than five years when they left for Spain with my brother and sister. My father took a job with an international moving company. I can't even remember if they asked me if I would have liked to come.

When I think about this strange time, it is difficult to remember the events in chronological order. At some point, I bought a secondhand motorcycle suit from a guy who became my good friend Fred Lefevere. I found out that his family was warm and friendly. They were Mormons, though that didn't mean much to me. I did understand that I felt at home there, and I knew I was welcome in their circle. Once my parents left, I spent a lot of time with them. Mr. Lefevere was a Sergeant Major in the Army, and, as a great bonus, Fred's sister Lia was beautiful and sweet. It wasn't long before Lia and I fell in love, and all my memories of that time are of one uninterrupted sunny spring day. I know that at the time, I was not clear on the distinction between wanting sex and feeling love, but one thing was very clear: for Mormons, there was absolutely no sex before marriage.

I finished high school in the beginning of the summer of 1974. I felt I was ready for real life and earning some real money. I wanted a profession with action and with lots of hands-on activity. My father had wanted me to become a policeman because he had been one during the war, and it had saved his life. But because of Mr. Lefevere's influence, I was more interested in joining the Army.

My friend Martin decided to go into the Army, Eddie chose to go into the Navy, and I chose to go into the communication division of the Army. It seemed a logical choice that took advantage of some of my interests and knowledge. When my father was working on his radio in our houseboat, I spent some of the money I had earned polishing shoes on buying my own supplies and building some of my own equipment. It meant that after the summer, I had to report to the Koninklijke Militaire School in the town of Weert. To my dismay, I realized that my first step in the military would begin again in a schoolroom.

I had only one moment of doubt. In those summer months, a film crew made up of hundreds of Americans and British people began to reconstruct a World War II battle. It was an odd sensation to see my father's past glamorized by Hollywood. When I found an ad in the paper announcing auditions for extras, I decided to live out one of my childhood fantasies of starring in a movie. I showed up and tried out, and for a few weeks, I dreamed about a career as an actor. When I was told that I could be an extra in the movie "A Bridge Too Far" I was thrilled, until I found out that it would interfere with my military career. After a long hard look at reality, I decided to give up on the acting fantasy and turned down the job.

I wore my military uniform when I married Lia, and we moved into an apartment at the Dubbelhof in Ede. Shortly after the ceremony, I had to go back to school in Weert. From that moment, we only saw each other on the weekends, but only when I had leave. We had trouble from the very beginning. As I went through basic training, she was all alone in the apartment. When I came back on the weekend, I was not the romantic fantasy that she had dreamed about while she was living in her protective parental home. We grew apart much faster than we had grown close. After about half a year, I told her it was over. She told me that she still loved me, but we both knew it would not be enough. Her tears and hurt feelings made me back off filing for divorce for another couple of months, and we pretended things might still work out.

Everything changed the moment Lia told me that she was pregnant. She confessed that she had not been taking the Pill for months and she had conceived. I was in a panic. I have no idea exactly what I said in that conversation, but I know that I must have used some choice words rarely heard in a proper Mormon household. Feeling equally panicked and disappointed, I packed my bags that very day and left.

I went to a lawyer (who later became a longtime friend) Tjeerd van Veen, and I told him the story. I explained to him that we had already discussed divorce and that I felt set up and trapped. Tjeerd wrote up a document in which Lia admitted that she had made the decision to become pregnant without my consent in order to tie me to her. I acknowledged from my side that I was the biological father, but added that I did not feel I had any responsibility. I would not acknowledge the child; I would not care for it and would not pay child support or alimony. On that basis, we got our divorce. When the child was born, I went to the hospital to show my respect. I considered Lia's decision irresponsible but also brave, and I understood that she faced a difficult future as a single mom. She called the baby Patrick, and as I watched him in his little bed, I asked myself if I felt anything for him. There was the biological reality—he really was my son—but I had no feelings towards him. In my eyes, he was a child like every other, and my short visit convinced me that my rational decision had been the correct one.

After that one visit, I never saw Patrick again. I did visit his grandparents, who made it clear to me that they liked me and had loved having me as a son-in-law. They sincerely wished things had turned out differently for their daughter, and of course, I agreed with them. Years later they told me about Patrick—that he was clearly my son and had inherited a bit of my character. During this same time, an uncle of mine let slip that my father had been married three times before he married my mother; it turned out that I have four or five siblings from those marriages. I guess it is "like father, like son" after all.

ONWARD

For while, it looked like the military might be a good life for me. It gave my life structure and order, which was a relief from the chaotic life I had experienced so far. The education I was getting was also practical, and that suited me well. But after about a year, I started feeling fed up—not just by the Army, but by the guys around me. It was my habit to work hard at everything; this made me a duck out of water in an environment where people were trying to do just enough to get by. I decided that civilian life would suit me better, so I left the Army.

In less than a month, I had a job in Amsterdam selling industrial-cleaning products for an American company called Certified Laboratories. Being a salesman is certainly a very different life than being a soldier, and I loved the challenge. It was my job to visit potential clients, demonstrate our products, and sell many as many vats of those cleaning products as I could. I knew nothing about cleaning, but learning how to clean something is not exactly difficult, so I caught on quickly. I had learned a thing or two about selling from my shoeshine days and from watching my father. I was happy to have a job, and I threw myself into the process. My enthusiasm was necessary because my salary was largely commission-based, but I did well and immediately began to earn a good income. My good life didn't last; I soon found out that the drums of cleaning products that were being delivered contained very a different product from the one that I was demonstrating. I felt like a swindler.

Mr. Gunther, my American boss, told me to stop whining. "You only see these people one time. You sell them the crap and you never see them again. Why the hell do you care?"

When I protested that I didn't like doing business that way, his answer was, "But Rudi, why do you care? You are a great salesperson!"

I quickly became disillusioned and decided that a life in sales was not my thing. Just as I had regretted dropping out of high school to become a stable boy and later decided to return to school, I now regretted leaving the Army and wanted to find a way back in.

But the Army did not want me back. Once you decide to leave, you are done, there is no going back. The most galling part was that I knew if I had stayed on, I would've been promoted to a position I would have enjoyed by now. I had blown it, and I was bereft.

One thing I had learned by then: you have to keep asking and keep looking for alternative ways to get what you want. It has always been my strong belief that you can always find something in the fine print; if you look hard enough, you will always find loopholes. If you can't get over the mountain, maybe you can go around or under it. Eventually I found the loophole I was looking for. I could not enlist, but a Dutch citizen has the right to serve in the military. When I walked in and asked to be drafted, they were astonished, but agreed that they could not refuse me. I wrote a letter to the Minister of Defense and asked him to draft me. I even managed to return to my old division where I served another two years.

After I left the Army for the second time, I started my first entrepreneurial venture called DeBo, which stood for Dekkers Boor ("Boor" is Dutch for "drill"). The business was based on a ridiculously simple concept. At the time, Holland had caught the do-it-yourself fever, and hardware stores were doing a brisk business. I found a factory in Germany that would sell me drill bits for less than two guilders. Since Dutch hardware stores were selling these very same drill bits for ten guilders, I had no problem selling them to the stores for 3.50 guilders, so everybody was happy. Because drill bits are small and I could transport hundreds of them in my car at a time, it was pretty lucrative. I was prosperous again and all was well. DeBo was a new beginning for me. It was the first time that I was in business for myself. My success convinced me that business was going to be my life.

During those years I had a fun bachelor lifestyle. After my short marriage with Lia I went through many girlfriends. All that changed the moment I met Astrid. I was still in the Army, and had taken a part-time job working for a taxi company. One magical evening, she stepped into my cab. We were both in our early twenties and we struck up a conversation. Astrid was a beautiful girl of Indonesian descent, with amazingly sexy, soft, dark-black hair down to her ass. She was a head shorter than I, slim as a reed, and had gorgeous eyes in which I could lose myself. Like a jerk, I did not ask her for a date right away, but I did a year-and-a-half later when I met her again by accident. When we began dating, Astrid worked in a nursing home. She was calm and very friendly to everybody. She was my opposite in almost every way, which was very attractive to me. She appreciated my interest and thought I was a suitable partner, but did not want to marry me. She didn't love me, she said, because she was in love with somebody in Paris. Maybe she did and maybe she didn't, but she was with me and stayed with me.

One day, I received a call informing me that my father had been in an accident. They had moved to Spain in 1976, and I hadn't seen them for many years. I will tell this story in more detail later on, but shortly after our visit there, my father died and I went back to Spain with Astrid. We stayed there for a year while I dealt with my mother and the issues around the inheritance. After a frustrating stay in Spain, Astrid and I moved back to Holland. It was ironic, after all those years in poverty, that the gift of the house in Ede was now a source of financial strife in our family.

On September 24, 1981, we became the proud and joyful parents of our sweet little Teressa. It was the most amazing experience of my whole life. This little one, this amazingly vulnerable little doll, was the perfect mixture of the two of us. I had become known for my cool, rational way of thinking, but all that disappeared with her birth. A week later, her mother and I got married.

I determined that I had to do something worthwhile to build a compelling future. My attitude was apparent to a real estate broker named Ton van de Bunt. I had walked into his office to buy some life insurance, since it didn't look like I would inherit much from my father's estate, and I wanted to make sure my daughter was well provided for in case of a disaster. Ton, who was the father of a friend of mine, was in charge of that office, a business that handled real estate and insurance.

Ton was a kind man, and he immediately told me that he was looking to hire people for his real estate business and asked if I was interested. I told him I would think about it for a few days because I had actually been thinking about starting another business of my own. After a week, I had not come up with anything more brilliant, so I accepted the job. Selling homes is a specialized skill, but in many ways, it was no different from selling drill bits and cleaning supplies. The biggest difference was that you really needed to be involved with your client. In the beginning, I thought that creating a rosy picture of the property and only lightly indicating the negative points of the house would give me the quickest sale. The first time I was confronted with a disappointed customer, I felt terribly guilty thinking about how I might have led them astray.

The exact opposite strategy was better for my conscience and turned out to be a better sales strategy, too. When I would show a property, I would immediately tell the customers all the negative factors. After I had shown them everything that was wrong with the house, I would start telling them all the positive points of the property. This honesty was appreciated by my clients; it made them feel like I was on their side. They knew they wouldn't be facing any big surprises, and they were more willing to deal with the inevitable drawbacks to the house. My income rose and after a short while, my little family was able to move into a beautiful home.

Things were going well but I always kept my eyes and ears wide open, my brain constantly working. Even now, I am always looking for solutions to practical problems and holes in the market, which is what happened with real estate. Once I figured out how the real estate business worked, I started my own company with my business partner Rob Sierenveld.

In the real estate business, selling existing homes is your main activity. Sellers sometimes walk into your business, but mostly you are sent listings of new houses with the multiple-listings system. After a couple of successful years with Rob, I decided to branch off on my own in the real estate field and started a new company, which I called Dekkers Malelaardij.

At that time, the real estate business was flat. You could make a decent living but there was no excitement. That, of course, did not please me, and I continued to look for new ways to make money. I soon realized that it was much more lucrative to buy a piece of land and build beautiful houses on speculation, or spec, which means you build a home before you have a buyer. I soon found my first opportunity in the town of Bennekom, where there were two properties that had been for sale for several years. I scooped them up, had my friend and architect Gijs ten Boske draw up plans for two beautiful houses, and bingo, I was in a new business.

From that moment on, I was a developer. I started small, with modest parcels of land, usually just one or two houses at a time. As time went along, the projects became larger. Eventually, I was building dozens of houses at a time. Gijs was my in-house architect. He would draw up variations on the basic design, one more beautiful than the next, which made potential buyers feel like they had great choices. Then I advertised complete packages, so that people could buy a parcel of land and the house, which I would then build for them. I delivered great quality for very reasonable prices. These days, inflation has made the quality houses I built at that time fabulous investments.

Because I could deliver a complete package and the business was running efficiently, I had a turnaround time of only a few months, which created a cash-flow machine. Every few months I was able to start up a new project. In theory, everything worked beautifully, but of course, there were times of immense financial stress. Real estate deals require huge amounts of money and not everybody is on time with their payments. Thank goodness I had a number of friends with good hearts (and who had no connection to organized crime) who were willing to make short-term loans. Gijs van Dijk was one, and also the Heiting family, whom I knew from my time spent cleaning out their stables. I paid them back as soon as I could possibly manage with generous interest, which ensured their willing cooperation the next time I was short.

In a few years, with an enormous amount of work, I managed to build a couple hundred homes. It pleases me to think that there are still thousands of people living in the houses that I developed and built. I employed many people in my town, including my good friend and lawyer, Arie de Leeuw. There were deals that had me working for weeks with only one hour of sleep a night. The pressure was immense, but my hard work and inventive deals paid off. By the time I was twenty-six, I had gone from poor boy from Amsterdam who barely got his high school diploma to living on a salary comparable to that of a brain surgeon.

During those years, I helped many of my friends make the leap to becoming property owners. A lot of them bought three or four apartments that they rented out: they are all still living high on the hog because of those investments. Though there were times when I had to work amazingly hard, I made a good income, even though I had to pay up to seventy-two percent of it in taxes to the Dutch government.

But my greatest joy was my growing family. Teressa acquired two little sisters, Dominique (March 24, 1985) and Leonara (June 14, 1987). They were beautiful children, with dark-blonde hair and subtly bronzed skin. Their bodies reminded me of young fawns, with soft, beautiful eyes like Bambi. I was proud of my children and proud that I could raise them in luxury, so they could grow up strong and healthy, both physically and emotionally. They had everything they ever needed or wanted: plenty of clothes, toys, food, and care. My own upbringing had been such a frightening example of how not to do things, and my parents had been uncaring and incapable. But we were doing it the right way. Because of my good income, my wife was able to devote all her loving energy to their care and education.

It wasn't all hard work though; I actually had time to become quite a good tennis player. One of the joys of having disposable income was that I could sponsor tennis tournaments. My competitive nature made me a good player, and I once had the pleasure and honor to play doubles with Tom Okker (a Dutch tennis champion in the sixties).

Not everything was quite as straight-forward as this narrative might make it sound. I very much believed, then and now, that you need to keep your rational mind functioning, even in emotional situations, and that you need to think through your decisions clearly. But my life has been saved on a few occasions by a totally different approach, and one of them happened around this time.

I was windsurfing on Lake Nulde. It was a cloudy day brought in by a hard blowing wind. I was having a great time going very fast, and then suddenly, without warning, I felt dizzy and fell off my board. I did not have a life vest on, in part because I am a strong swimmer and in part because I was an arrogant young man. I cannot even remember going under. The first thing I became conscious of was that I was floating gently and that I was perfectly warm. It felt as if someone was holding me, as if I was feeling the perfect fantasy of being held safely in my mother's arms. It was a fantastic feeling, all warm and fuzzy, and I wanted it to go on and on.

Then it dawned on me that this was all wrong and could not possibly be happening. I suddenly remembered that I had been windsurfing and fallen which meant that I was in the water and ought to be cold. Then I fully woke up out of the dream, or whatever that was, and realized I was underwater. Luckily, I saw light above me, which I knew must be sunlight telling me which way to swim. I did not realize in that moment that this would have been impossible because of the heavy cloud cover that blocked all direct sunlight that day.

I started to swim toward the light and then heard a voice in my head saying, "Do not swim to the light; swim down." I don't know why I listened to that voice, but I swam toward the dark and a few seconds later I was on top of the water. I could not find my board, but I let the current carry me to shore. I never had an explanation for what happened, but listening to that voice saved my life, and it would do so on several more occasions.

FLYING

If I look at it objectively, it is perhaps logical that after bicycles, motorcycles, and lots of cars, I would one day try to fly airplanes. It might be logical in retrospect, but the thought actually never entered my mind. What happened is that somebody invited me for a flight, and with that one experience I was hooked.

In the mid-eighties, I met Tom Furstenberg, one of the owners of Samsonite. His ex-wife and their son had moved into one of my houses, and Tom made a point of driving over in his Maserati to thank me personally for taking such good care of them. That was the beginning of our friendship. One day he casually asked me if I would like to fly with him to London in his brand-new Piper Seneca, a twin-engine plane. It seemed like a fun thing to do, so I agreed, with no idea what that trip would spark in me. During the flight, Tom explained to me how things worked. By the time we had reached our cruising altitude, we were flying at about 170 knots per hour, and I was impressed. The ease with which Tom talked to me and flew the airplane at the same time was deceptive. We were flying smoothly and in perfect balance, as if we were on a little boat on a big lake with no wind to stir us. This calm was broken the very moment I put my hands on the controls. I can remember exactly how it felt to have the controls in my hands that day, and how my miserable, amateurish attempt at keeping the plane level resulted in a roller coaster ride that made me nauseous. As badly as I was doing, this did not detract from the heady sensation of absolute freedom.

By the time we returned to Holland, I was sold. I immediately enrolled in flying classes at Rob van der Sightenhorst's flight school in the town of Teuge. Not only did I want to learn how to fly, but I also wanted to have my own airplane just like Tom. And just like Tom, I wanted to have a Piper Seneca. It's not a cheap plane, but it was definitely something to brag about. Since I worked hard and had some money, I could afford it.

The difficulty in learning how to fly is very similar to that of learning how to drive a car. Once the car is driving on a straight road and you have things under control, it is not all that challenging. The hard parts are at the beginning and the end of the trip: maneuvering the car into traffic and learning how to squeeze into that perfect parking spot. Flying is the same thing. Taking off and landing are the most difficult pieces to master. To get your commercial license in the Netherlands, you have to fly two-hundred hours and you have to pass several exams, both oral and written. You have to fly solo, you have to fly at night, you have to fly in bad weather, and there is quite a bit of studying required for the written exam. Obviously, you have to pass all parts of the exam, and there are no shortcuts. Requirements are similar in other countries with some minor modifications.

Rob, the owner of the flight school, was a nice guy. At some point he became my friend and a long time later, he even came to visit me in America. As nice as he was, when it came to flying, Rob was a tough teacher. He left no stone unturned in his effort to make you a good pilot, and if he thought you couldn't do it, he had no problem throwing you out. After a while, he saw that I had some talent for flying, but my landings, to put it mildly, were my weak spot. I had no problem taking off, I loved flying in the air, but my landing approaches were always either too shallow or too steep. As with so much else, the solution was practice, practice, practice. One day Rob took me in his Cessna 172 and all we did was take off and land, over and over again. I must have landed thirty times that day and by the time we were done, I knew exactly how to navigate the crosswinds, how to position the flaps perfectly, and how much power to give. The result of this intensive training is that I am still known for my excellent, soft landings.

Business was good and I bought my first plane: a Cessna 172 with proud call numbers PH-RBR on the tail. I bought it secondhand from the Dutch airline KLM, and I glowed with pride. Astrid didn't want to go flying, but my friends loved it and I often treated them to free rides. However, my greatest joy was flying solo. No feeling can match the feeling you get when you find yourself 1,000 feet above the earth, literally as free as a bird. At no time and in no place was I so completely at peace, so deeply in touch with my very center, as behind the controls of my Cessna.

When I was not flying my airplane, the flight school

was allowed to use the plane as a rental in return for free lessons. I was already planning my future purchase of that Piper Seneca, but I did not yet have the license to fly a plane of that size. Renting my Cessna was paying for the lessons I needed to get the additional lessons. Even though there are quite a few flying enthusiasts in the Netherlands, relatively few people own their own plane, perhaps no more than about two-hundred individuals, which meant there was no problem finding customers.

After a little bit of market research, I found that buying a Piper Seneca would cost about three times as much in Holland as it would in the United States. It didn't take much to decide the obvious solution was to go to the United States and buy my plane there. I contacted J&S Aircraft, an airplane dealership in Naples, Florida. Scotty Ulring owned the business with her brother and husband Joel, and she flew me back and forth across the United States to find my perfect plane. In the end, we found her in Rawlings, Wyoming. Scotty declared it "technically perfect." I even loved the call number N2832L, (NL is the abbreviation for the Netherlands) so I paid for the plane, and we flew it back to Naples. I was jazzed.

Now I had to get the plane to Europe, but I wasn't even licensed to fly it. Even after I got my license, there was no way I had the experience to embark on such a complicated and dangerous transatlantic voyage. Thank goodness that was not an obstacle for my friend Tony Ossendorp, a captain with KLM. He readily agreed to fly the plane back with me to Holland. I got my plane ready for its voyage by installing an extra gas tank.

I also rented a communication and VHF transmitter, which was installed right behind the passenger seat.

On our first leg, we had minor problems with the plane over Massachusetts, but we only needed to replace an alternator. It was a short delay and not a big deal. It felt good, actually; we got the bugs out of the system and now we knew we could depend on our plane for the long stretch over open water.

There are two routes that you can fly between the United States and Europe: a northerly one over Iceland and Greenland and a southerly one via the Azores and Portugal. The first leg of this journey had us fly over land, to St. John's, Newfoundland; at that point, we had to make our choice between these two routes. We pored over the weather reports and chose the southerly route, even though we had to fly over a huge stretch of water, about 1,200 miles. In those days, before the general availability of GPS, that was a tricky bit of navigation. Even now, with GPS navigation, you are no longer allowed to make the trip without a dingy, for safety reasons.

From St. John's, we would fly to Santa Maria in the Azores. On such a long-distance trip, even a one-degree miscalculation will make you miss the entire island. The real trick is dealing with the cross winds, which inevitably blow you off your ideal trajectory. We could not afford many mistakes, because even with the extra tank, we only had enough fuel for an additional sixty miles.

The morning we left from St John's, the weather was beautiful, and I had absolute confidence in Tony's ability to get us there. Three quarters of the way into the flight, we hit some unexpected turbulence, and I hit my head against the radio mounted behind my seat. My hard head did not suffer much, but it broke our radio. I didn't find out until we landed that the malfunction was a loose contact in the microphone—all I knew is that we were now without radio contact. Up to that point, I had faithfully radioed New York our position every five degrees, and now we were without that lifeline. In desperation, I started looking outside, hoping to find where we needed to land in Azores. It was, of course, much too early to do so, but in my panic, I did not know what else to do. Tony noticed how nervous I was and tried to calm me down, saying, "Relax, Rudi, I know we are on the right course. I studied the charts, I know the winds, and I've verified our speed. I'm sure everything is okay."

Cold comfort. There we were, flying over the Atlantic, and as far as the eye could see, there was no land. It's not that I doubted his calculations, but without the confirmation of people who could consult the radar screen, there was no way to absolutely know for sure. The disaster scenario was that we would run out of fuel while still in the middle of the ocean. Tony was just as aware of that as I was, but his long experience had taught him a great deal more self-control. I kept trying the radio and suddenly there was a voice. I heaved a sigh of relief; the tower told me that they had just begun to organize a rescue mission for us. We had been off the air so long that they had assumed we had crashed. He sounded amazingly cool and businesslike; it was clear that they had not been as nervous as I was. We found Santa Maria without a problem and landed at the airport. We prepared ourselves for the next leg, but after the long transatlantic trip, that little hop to Porto in Portugal was a snap. The next leg would be even easier, over the Pyrenees, straight through France and Belgium to my home, sweet home. The weather looked great, the route was a comforting, over-land trip, and we were almost home.

The next leg from Santa Maria to Porto in Portugal was a mere six hours over water. It was an easy trip with no problems. As usual, we studied the weather maps the next day and saw it was perfectly clear between Portugal and the Netherlands. We took off and started our trip filled with optimism, flying over the breathtaking Pyrenees at 10,000 feet.

To my left, above the Gulf of Biscay, I suddenly saw a flash. It was beautiful and fascinating but did not concern me; the weather map had not predicted bad weather, and the Gulf of Biscay was far away. I asked Tony if he had noticed the flash, and he said in a cool, unconcerned voice that he had seen it. When I saw the next flash, I asked again if he had noticed, and if it was lightning. He laughed, shook his head, and said confidently, "Of course that's not lightning. The Gulf is used for military training, and though they shoot blanks, it does give off a flash. That must be what we are seeing."

Since Tony had also flown in the Navy and had been a full captain for many years at KLM, I assumed that he knew better than I did. I am suspicious and careful, but not stupid, and I have enormous respect for professionals. I was still unconcerned when we flew into light clouds about half-an-hour later.

Then the clouds thickened, the air turned darker,

and the turbulence increased. Suddenly the turbulence increased a lot, and in a short time, we were confronted with upward drafts of about 8,000 feet per minute and downward drafts of 15,000 feet per minute. We went up and down like a yoyo. A few times, we even turned over and Tony expertly turned the plane back to its horizontal position. During one such jolt, I bumped my head against the radio for the second time, but this time I lost consciousness for ten seconds.

When I regained consciousness, I saw the most frightening sight I had ever seen: Tony did not have his hands on the controls. He was literally not flying the plane anymore. When he saw that I was conscious again, he shouted over all the noise, "I have to let the storm do its thing. If I try to counter these forces, we will die. The plane cannot handle two contrary forces of this magnitude, so if I do something, I'll break the plane." I had never heard of such an absurd thing in all my life, but I had no time to wonder about it because the plane was going through the most unbelievable gyrations. We were a toy being tossed about in the power of the storm, which felt very different from the sweet feeling of freedom in flying. This was a nightmare unlike any I had ever experienced.

On the radio, we heard somebody say that there was a Cumulus Nimbus cloud of 60,000 feet. Any self-respecting pilot would avoid such a cloud like the plague as it would be dangerous in the extreme. The center of this cloud consists of a strong upward draft of warm air. Gliders love flying underneath such clouds (though never one this large) because they can take advantage of the upward motion. However, the outer part of the cloud has strong downward forces, and we were being tossed around by both conflicting forces in turn.

To make matters worse, we were hit by lightning and I had to shut down the radio. In theory, you will not be hurt by a lightning bolt in the sky, just as you are not hurt by a lightning bolt hitting a car with good rubber tires. The effect is called the Cage of Faraday, in which the charge is absorbed by the metal hull of the airplane, but the passengers inside are safe. You have to allow time for the charge to dissipate before you get out of the airplane to be sure you do not get a shock. The more immediate danger is the brilliance of the lightning, which can permanently damage the retina of your eye and cause blindness, so Tony advised me to keep my eyes closed. I had no problem doing that because I'd never been so scared in my life. I thought this was the end, and I know Tony did too.

Just when I thought it could not get worse, it did. When I peeked through my eyes, I saw a fireball of at least three feet in diameter. It was a blue ball of pure light called St. Elmo's Fire, an amazing electrical phenomenon that sometimes occurs during a thunderstorm, which rolled over the left wing, jumped over the left motor to the right motor, and over to the right wing. It was a beautiful fireworks display but I was in no position to enjoy it. The ball disappeared to the back of the plane and out of view as the static electricity crackled and danced over the windows.

The storm was not finished with us yet. We were tossed about so much that right side up and upside down no longer had meaning to us. The ordeal seemed to take hours, though we later calculated that the entire event must have taken only eight or nine minutes in real time. Our nerves were tested to the maximum and we were exhausted from tension and fear. I suddenly saw a lighter area in the clouds. I pointed it out to Tony, but he had already seen the same thing. He gently maneuvered the plane in that direction, which appeared to be a hole in the cloud. The moment we went through that hole all our troubles were solved. Directly below us was the airport of Bordeaux. Tony landed the plane immediately, and after a few minutes of taxiing, I got out. The moment my feet touched the sweet, stable, predictable earth, I fell to my knees. I kissed her and thanked her for being her predictable, stable self.

My sleep that night was filled with nightmares and my love for flying had completely evaporated.

"I'm not going up," I told Tony the next morning over breakfast. "Not now and not ever. I am completely done with aviation."

"Nothing doing," said Tony, unperturbed. "I'm flying and you are going with me. What happened to us yesterday was unique. You'll never have an experience like that again in your life. Since you had it now, you know you're done!"

My rational mind told me that it was inescapable logic, and in retrospect, I am very thankful for his words. Without his insistence, I would have never considered a career in aviation. Against all expectations, and because of Tony's wise decisions, the airplane did not look as if she suffered any damage. We checked it out thoroughly, but, miracle of miracles, nothing was broken. The flight to Holland was uneventful, which was fine with me.

Though we flew halfway around the world, we never had any problems with customs until we came to my local airport of Teuge, Holland. We had not even gotten out of the plane and customs agents were already standing in front of us, screaming. We had just flown for ten hours straight, so we were exhausted and I was not in the mood for nonsense.

I said, "Excuse me?"

They barked again, "Get out of the plane. We want to investigate the plane right now."

I answered, "Listen, I'm not even out of the plane. Why are you yelling at me?"

The guy wouldn't simmer down, so I continued, "Sir, get out of my way right now, or I will start the plane and leave. I have not put my feet on Dutch soil, and inside this plane, this is still America, and you can't do anything. I've just flown halfway around the world. Nobody gave me any problems until I got here. I am a Dutch citizen, and I come back to my own country, and my own hometown, and my own airfield, and you bitch me out like this?"

They realized the absurdity of their behavior and backed off. They apologized and told me they would wait for me in the office. A few minutes later, I walked into the office and said the plane was ready for their inspection. Everything was fine, of course.

This trip cured me of ever wanting to fly through clouds. I do have my Instrument Flight Rules (IFR) license, which means if the weather is bad or there is limited visibility, I can fly using only my instruments to guide me. But ever since that life-threatening experience, I stay on the ground if it looks like it will thunder. I will never voluntarily put myself in that position again. My respect for Mother Nature and her power is enormous; I probably owe my life to never underestimating the forces at work.

For years I was the proud owner of that Piper, and after I got the appropriate license to fly her, it always brought me much pleasure.

Our departure to America in 1991 forced me to sell her. Coincidentally, the buyer, whom I had never met, and I had the same last name. Ad Dekkers could tell that I was truly sad to get rid of her. He was a kind man and said he would be happy to let me fly her on a farewell trip. He said that he flew to Switzerland regularly and promised to let me know the next time he went.

About six months later, he finally called and invited me to accompany him on a flight to Switzerland the following Saturday. I had been looking forward to the trip over the beautiful Alps and accepted immediately, full of excitement about a trip in my beloved plane. All that excitement somehow evaporated over the next couple of days; when he called to confirm the time, I had lost all appetite for the trip. I could not rationally explain why it felt wrong, but I did not want to fly to Switzerland that Saturday. I felt like a jerk, but I made up a phony excuse and begged off. I never heard from him again, and I figured he was mad at me for canceling at the last minute.

In 1999, I was flying from Amsterdam to Miami with Martinair, and ran into an old acquaintance of mine.

We talked for a while, exchanging news and general aviation gossip.

He turned to me and asked, "That old Seneca, wasn't that one of your planes?"

I glowed with the happy memory. "Yeah, that Seneca was mine. How is that beautiful plane?"

There was a moment of painful silence. "Are you telling me you don't know what happened?" he asked with a shocked face. I said I had never heard anything more about my plane, and he told me the strangest story. Ad Dekkers had flown to Switzerland with my old plane and had flown into a mountain. He had been killed in the crash, the plane completely destroyed on the very same trip I had been invited to take with him.

Later I saw an archive photo of the newspaper article that gave me the chills. Unlike the time when I fell off my windsurfer, I had not heard a voice. This time it had been my gut telling me to back off. I had listened and it had saved my life.

TO AMERICA AND BACK

At thirty-five, I felt that I had reached the limit of what I could accomplish in the Netherlands. I had proven myself as a builder and developer. Though we are all fallible, I felt I was a successful father and head of household. I didn't appreciate the Dutch attitude that it was wrong for me to be rich, or the huge taxes I had to pay as punishment for being successful, even though I worked very hard for every cent. Even minor things began to annoy me, including the dreary, cold, and rainy Dutch weather.

Buying my plane was my first introduction to America. We visited many times after that, and with each visit, I liked the country more. The huge, wide-open spaces and breathtaking natural beauty are so different from the cramped and mostly urbanized Dutch landscape. Perhaps the most charming aspect of America is its people. Americans tend to be open and friendly, and not jealous. They are happy if you are successful, they are not terribly prejudiced, and they behave civilly in traffic.

Yes, I know, there are also plenty of arrogant, prejudiced, narrow, aggressive people in the United States.

But you have to remember, I am only comparing the US to the Netherlands, not to some absolute heaven-on-earth ideal. For instance, when Dutch people visit the United States for the first time, they judge the behavior of salespeople to be absurdly servile. They feel like the employees are bowing too deeply and being too friendly; to the cold Dutch, this type of service makes a phony impression. It doesn't feel like that to me, but even if it were true, I prefer the superficial friendliness and ease of the Americans to the chilly, often nasty attitude of the Dutch.

This is how I see it: ninety-five percent of all the people you meet are not your intimate friends. They are the people you meet in the street, in the supermarket, in an elevator, or in the waiting room at the doctor's office. What do I care if none of these people qualify for my intimate friendship? I am happy that they are friendly, that they seem prepared to help me, and that there is a general atmosphere of cooperation. I love to strike up a conversation with the stranger standing next to me and have that person respond in a friendly way. To me, even superficial hospitality is worth its weight in gold.

But I have to admit, after all these years in America, I have not developed any truly deep friendships with Americans. I did not move to the US until I was in my thirties, an age when it is much more difficult to make new friends. My best friends are Dutch, most of them from my youth. I have found that many other people also hold on to the friendships they made in their youth, and I find those to be the strongest ones, so maybe that is not unusual. However, for my everyday life, I'm happy to surround myself with friendly Americans, which was the real reason I wanted to move to America.

Of course, there were other reasons as well. The fabulous climate in Florida was very appealing to the entire family. Also, America is generally a much more business-friendly country. Overall, it seemed to me that it was time to emigrate. I sold Dekkers Malelaardij to Bert van Engelehoven Jr., the son of my first steady employer. We packed up our stuff, and the Dekkers family prepared to move.

Despite our enthusiasm, our first move to Florida in 1988 turned out to be premature. My idea was that I would do the same work in America I had succeeded at in Holland. I immediately bought a couple of parcels of land, and I was planning to building spec houses. But with more than a thousand real estate agents in Florida, trying to create a real estate and building business was an uphill battle. Within a year, we moved back to Holland and rented an apartment in Renkum, not far from where I had grown up and built my real estate business. If our initial move to America was premature, then our return to Holland was too hasty. The adjustment to America had simply needed a bit more time; I now realize that this was the typical back-and-forth move that I had done so often in my life. Back in the Netherlands, we prepared again for the move back to America where we did finally make our permanent home in 1993.

During those first few months in America, I had also found a new kind of business that appealed to me. I had met the owners of Computer Connections in Naples, and had seen their great success with the personal computer. The market penetration of the PC was a lot further along in America than it was in the Netherlands at that time, and IBM was the market leader in Holland. The IBM computers were fantastic, but were also very expensive, and Dutch taxes made them unaffordable for most people. That meant there was a hole in the market, and I decided to enter into the same business that Michael Dell would later grow into an empire. I started to import computer components from America and assemble them in the Netherlands. The name for the company was Import American Computers, which I abbreviated to Impac.

In those days, IBM sold their computers for 4,000 Dutch guilders, but for a little more than half the price, I could deliver clones of comparable quality. I was confident I would conquer the market and went full speed ahead. To my huge surprise, I was completely wrong. I just couldn't sell them. A little bit of research showed me why people were willing to pay nearly twice as much for an IBM—they offered a two-year guarantee. Moreover, it was a guarantee people were willing to trust because of the stability and reputation of their name. I had no problem coming up with a strategy to overcome that hurdle. I was willing to give them the computer for half the money down and allow the rest to be paid on a monthly basis with no interest over two years. In effect, it would give them the same two-year IBM guarantee.

That strategy worked like a dream, and soon I was selling hundreds of PCs a month. Because everything was running so well, I started a second company called

Intelec. A few years later, I was bought out by Royal Borsumij Wehry, a large publicly held company. As part of the buyout, I started working for Borsumij, but after a while that ended unhappily and absurdly amidst huge misunderstandings.

It was now 1993 and the American dream was still alive and well in the Dekkers household. It seemed to be the right moment to make our return to America, and this time we were better prepared. Because of all of my business dealings, I was already in America about half the time so the move was not so dramatic for me. For my wife and daughters, it was a bigger transition, but they loved the United States and were ready for the challenge. For a while, we lived in a rental home in Naples. As it turned out, we had no trouble at all adjusting this time, since America is such a user-friendly consumer paradise. Astrid found that when she went to the supermarket she was already familiar with most of the brands because they were advertised in the Netherlands. The children already spoke a little bit of English, and they soon felt at home, participating in school activities, going out to eat, riding on a school bus. Everything was new and fun. They wanted to belong, and very soon they did.

In some ways, my career life began to look as checkered as that of my father, except that I succeeded in everything I tried. My attitude was and is simply this: just let me look around and I'll figure it out. I'm a quick learner, I work really hard, but once I master something, I start to get bored. That's not true for very many people, and don't have what it takes to move on. But I only have this one life, and I have no intention of being bored.

My new company in the United States, International Computer Product, exported computer memory and hard drives to the Netherlands. I soon found people who were willing to sell them in the Netherlands, and they were selling fabulously. However, I quickly found out that they were selling my products for less than they were buying them from me. I decided to confront the situation head on and called my business partners.

They laughed and asked me: "Have you never wondered why we kept changing our business names?"

I answered innocently, "It really makes no difference to me what you call yourself."

But their fraudulent scheme lay in this little detail. In Holland, there is a nineteen percent value-added tax. On the invoice, they were selling their wares cheaply, adding that nineteen percent, and that was the customer's price. However, they never paid that tax to the Dutch government. By the time the IRS caught up with them, they would let the company go bankrupt and start up a new company. It was a dirty trick and I was shocked. In the Netherlands it is a national sport to pay as little in taxes as possible, just as it is in the United States, but this was outright tax fraud.

I should have immediately gotten out of the business at that point. I should have listened to my internal sense of right and wrong, and I should have taken my own outrage more seriously. However, as a businessperson, I had learned to use my rational thinking to protect my business interests. I called my American lawyer and asked him if I was doing anything wrong. His advice was very clear: "They are committing tax fraud, but you are doing nothing wrong. All you do is deliver the goods, right? Just keep paying your taxes in the USA, and keep proper records like you have been doing."

I was glad for the advice, because it was a lucrative business. But making the decision to continue this business for another month, even though it was on the advice of my lawyer, was one of the stupidest things I've ever done in my life. It was stupid, because once I knew a crime was being committed, I was culpable. I had never in my life done anything criminal; I might have been clever, but I never deliberately did anything illegal. To this day, I am sorry I continued for that month.

A little while later, a shipment was confiscated. After that, the business dissolved. About a year later, the Dutch tax officials from FIOD (Fiscale Inlichtingen-en Opsporingsdienst, the Dutch equivalent of the IRS) in charge of investigating tax fraud came to visit me in Naples. I cooperated fully and offered to come to Holland for further investigation. I have to admit that I was so horrified to announce myself to FIOD that I first went for a walk around my native Amsterdam to gather some courage. I went in after a few hours of aimless wandering, and then sat through four days of inquiries at their main office in Hoofddorp, about thirty kilometers or twenty miles west of Amsterdam. I have to admit that the people at FIOD were considerate and nice. They did their best to make the questioning as efficient as possible and to make my stay pleasant. All the horror stories I had heard in Holland about the FIOD turned out to be complete nonsense. They were just people trying to do a good job.

The only problem was that I was now officially a co-conspirator and possibly even a main suspect, since my nice colleagues in what was now called a "criminal organization" pointed the finger at me as the main guy. According to their papers, I embezzled up to $30 million. In stark contrast to that $30 million I was supposed to have stolen, my earnings from the computer business, including my salary, was not far from the break-even point. If you include the shipment that was confiscated and the shipment that was stolen by one of my colleagues, there was precious little to show for all of my work and trouble.

When I told the investigators that they shouldn't try to play us against each other, they suddenly decided they had developed a desperate need for a leisurely cup of coffee and they "accidentally" forgot to take their files with them. They gave me plenty of time to read what my coworkers had said about me. Even my good friend, the lawyer Arie, with whom I had done so many real estate deals in the past, accused me. From that moment on, the FIOD was assured of my absolute and complete cooperation: I have no pity on people who try to screw me.

As far as I was concerned, it was perfectly clear that my business partners had charged their customers the appropriate taxes, but had failed to pay those taxes to the government. I will never forget that day in court. The state attorney accused me of embezzling tax money. There was an immediate request to have me held in prison until there was a decision, since I was considered a flight risk. The three judges went into a private conference, and I looked to Tjeerd, who was my lawyer and a good friend who always stood by me.

He said to me, "As your lawyer, I advise you to leave now. You are a free man; you were not even under compulsion to be present. However, once those judges come back, that might be a different story. You have your freedom right now, so get out." Until that moment, it had never even occurred to me to escape. After all, I had come here on my own dime, all the way from America to be at this hearing. But now that I was being threatened with jail time, I considered it, and with my heart thumping in my chest I walked out of the courtroom with as much dignity as I could muster. In the hallway I increased my pace, and when I saw the front door, I started to run. I ran through the town at quite a clip and didn't stop until my mobile phone went off. It was my lawyer telling me that the judges had decided not to put me in jail, and I could come back safely.

Their judgment came six agonizingly long weeks later; the judges found me guilty. My penalty was either a million guilders or one year in jail. According to Tjeerd, this was simply not possible. He insisted that the statute of limitations had run out the previous year and that the judges had simply not reviewed their paperwork carefully enough. We decided to appeal, and he was sure I would be acquitted.

It took the FIOD more than five years to get the case in front of a judge. Not until July 1999 was there a hearing at the court in Haarlem, a city twenty kilometers or twelve miles west of Amsterdam. I was worried about the case all those years because I had no idea what was going to happen, but Tjeerd assured me that nothing could happen to me because the statute of limitations had run out in this case.

I did not come from America to attend that appeal. I guess I had learned my lesson. The original sentence was thrown out, and to this day I don't have a criminal record.

THE FLYING BUSINESS

Soon after my move to the United States in 1993, I bought a Beechcraft Duke, a six-seat twin-engine plane that looks like a jet. Buying that plane required making contact with the people who repair planes; all airlines require a great deal of maintenance. I was fortunate enough to meet Dan Smith, who is both a nice guy and an amazing mechanic who can fix planes that other people have given up on. Soon I was getting requests from other owners who wanted Dan to work on their planes, and I knew that I had a business in the making. I created an agreement with Dan at the end of 1993 to form a plane repair company in Naples I called Aerojet Service Center Inc, DBA Ambassador Airways, or Ambassador for short. I thought converting the overhead costs of my airplane repairs into a source of income was a smart idea, but it would only work if I was prepared to put an incredible amount of time and energy into getting the shop off the ground. I worked smart instead of just hard whenever I could.

I rented a 10,000 square feet hanger and hired Dan as my head mechanic. Eventually nine of his colleagues did their work there as well. As Ambassador grew, we added services including flying lessons, plane rentals, and the option for owners to have their planes serviced with us. Naples is a very rich town; it has about as many private plane owners as all of Holland combined, so my repair business grew quickly.

The FAA had officially endorsed us as a "145 repair station," which meant that we were delivering the highest quality service. Though we reached the highest pinnacle there, I could not say the same of our flight school. According to the Federal Aviation Regulations, which administrates the law as far as flight schools are concerned, we were designated an FAR-61. Simply put, our instruction was not first-rate quality and we were not a fully accredited institution. This was critical because it made attracting students very difficult.

I thought long and hard about how I could get more students. I knew Americans would be hard to attract because my designation would not allow me to provide the training necessary for FAA licenses. In Europe, they had passed a new law that required all pilots to get a JAR license (Joint Aviation Regulation), which was difficult to get because of all the new rules. This license was also so expensive that European flight schools were motivated to send their students overseas to log the hours they needed. European students would get up to speed here, then finish training at their local flight schools, where they could take the licensing exams. I decided that my business would target those Europeans, and contacted Tony Gunn, an English gentleman, who set up all the necessary paperwork and processes for us to become an approved JAR flight school. He became my new chief flight instructor and JAR examiner. We were one of only three schools in the USA who could offer this designation, so we were in a great position to do some good business. After years of marketing efforts, I also finally landed a contract with the SFT flight school in England, which sent me about twenty students a month. The future of Ambassador looked pretty rosy at that point. By 1999, I was employing ten mechanics and twenty flight instructors.

But Ambassador did not turn a profit for the first seven years. The sad but true joke in the aviation industry is that if you want to make one million, you have to start with two million. I had a decent salary, and there were increasingly more people who made their living working for my company, but the margins in the airplane industry were very slim. It took years of hard work to build my business from the ground up. There were times we were not able to pay the bills on time, which caused some aggravation. But as a foreigner, I couldn't get bank loans, which severely limited my options. Of course, I met all my financial obligations and in 2000 I was finally turning a profit.

Once Ambassador was up and running, I started to look around for a new business venture. My next business practically fell in my lap. I met Stan Huffman on the golf course. He was into his seventies and owned a flight school with his son. Stan was thinking about retiring, and his son did not want to continue the business, so he was considering selling his school. I told him I was interested and we set up a time for me to look at it. My first visit to Huffman Aviation left me very impressed. Though the buildings were old, he owned them outright, and the grounds were well maintained. Huffman Aviation had more buildings than Ambassador, a larger hangar, more planes, and more personnel.

What made Huffman Aviation especially desirable were their two crown jewels. The first was the documentation that designated Huffman as an FAR 141 flight school with full accreditation. This meant that foreign students were able to get their student visas approved when they enrolled at his school. This was very attractive to foreign students training for an FAA license. The second jewel was the fuel pump. Stan Huffman had acquired the paperwork necessary to store and sell fuel. It was a tremendous savings in terms of fueling his own planes. It also attracted many other clients and was a great source of income.

It did not take me long to decide that I wanted to buy Huffman Aviation. It was a very interesting business with lots of possibilities I thought I could exploit. The only problem was coming up with the cash to buy it since I still did not qualify for bank loans. The solution came from one of my customers. I had quite a few interesting if not eccentric clients, including Wally Hilliard, who had been taking flying lessons since 1996. Occasionally, Wally said something that aroused my curiosity. For instance, one day he looked at a Pilatus PC 12, a single-engine turboprop plane made in Switzerland that can be used as a nine-seat standard passenger airliner or a six-to-eight-seat executive corporate plane. It was fueling up at our pumps, and he made an offhand comment that he would like to own such a plane. I had a good laugh and forgot about it, because I knew that such a plane costs about two million dollars.

One fine day, out of the blue, Wally gave me a check for $100,000. It was odd, and even though I had many good places to put that money, I let the check sit in my bureau drawer. I expected it might be a joke or a mistake, and he would want it back. After about a week, I called him and asked him why he gave me that check. His answer was a matter-of-fact and calm "I know you can use it."

I had just gotten out of the computer business and I still owed back taxes. Ambassador was not very big; I only had two planes at the time. I was really in need of a cash infusion and I guess Wally had seen that. He told me he trusted my business sense.

I still had my suspicions and asked him, "What if my business tanks and I lose your money?"

"Big deal," he answered, "I earn that in one day."

When I heard that, I immediately cashed the check. He was very bright and very well informed about business in general. Even though he was in his seventies, he had just retired. He and a friend had founded one of the biggest health insurance companies in the United States and sold it when they had 6,000 employees.

Wally lived in his beautiful three million dollar home in Naples during the winter months and spent the rest of the year in what was probably a larger home in Wisconsin. Once I realized that he had a huge amount of money to play with, I immediately set about finding him a Pilatus PC 12.

Wally really believed in me and offered himself as a source of investment money. He literally said to me, "You can use my fortune!" I decided to go to him with my ideas about Ambassador, and with his help, the business grew much more quickly than it would have otherwise. Wally and I became friends and would later become formal business partners. I did eventually find a Pilatus for him, as well as a Lear jet a few years later. Because of Wally's support and financial backing, I had no hesitation about negotiating a sale price with Stan Huffman.

With Wally's capital as a guarantee, I borrowed 1.2 million from the bank, which made me the owner of Huffman aviation in 1999, the only Fixed Base Operation—a service center located at an airport and known as an FBO for short—at the airport in Venice. It had a flight school with twenty planes, a maintenance division, several buildings, and a gas pump. The business did about 1.5 million per year and I had good hopes that I could double that in the next two years.

Now I was really busy. I had two companies, both of which were in a growth phase, and they were about 125 miles apart. It was nearly impossible to be in both places every day with the legal speed limit on the highway of sixty-five miles per hour. Even if I hit no traffic, I would spend four hours commuting every day. The obvious solution was to become a licensed helicopter pilot. So I did just that, and then I bought a helicopter. Now it took me twenty minutes to drive from my home to the airfield. It would take another twenty minutes via helicopter to Venice and I could spend most of my time at Huffman. If necessary, I could fly another twenty-five minutes to Ambassador to finish my workday there. Now that my time was being used so much more efficiently, I often could get home in the late afternoon and fit in a round of golf at the end of the day.

Helicopter flying came with its own adventures. One time, I was flying my helicopter with Patrick, an airplane instructor who did not fly helicopters, as a passenger. An engine went out over the Everglades, close to the site of the tragic ValuJet crash of 1996. I managed to land on a little island in the Everglades, cooled the motor off, and eventually got it started again. We lifted off and started to fly back toward Naples when suddenly we smelled smoke in the cockpit. I thought the motor was on fire, but now there was no place to land. Pat panicked and screamed, "We're on fire; we're going to crash!"

I was more worried about crash landing in the swamp, where we could drown or be eaten by alligators or crocodiles (since southern Florida is the only place in the world where they are both found) than I was about an engine fire. I told him, "As long as this thing is flying, I'm going to keep her in the air." I kept flying in the direction of I-75, which was only a few miles away. I thought I could make it. Everything I checked was fine, including the oil pressure.

My biggest immediate problem was the smoke coming into the cockpit. Although I was technically flying away from the smoke, the wind flowing around the helicopter was pushing it back into the cockpit. In thirty seconds, the smoke got so bad that I couldn't see. I decided to fly sideways instead, which effectively blew the smoke out of the cockpit. Despite all the thick, smelly smoke, I still didn't see a fire, so I kept flying and checking my instruments. We finally made it to I-75 and landed the helicopter in a rest area. I turned off the motor to let it cool down and Pat immediately jumped out in complete panic.

After all that drama, the problem turned out to be minor. The cockpit is separated from the motor of the turbine by a firewall that is little more than a heat-resistant blanket. The turbine had gotten so hot that the firewall was smoking. The only damage was a hole in the blanket, but it had certainly created a heck of a lot of smoke. It had not been dangerous—really more of a nuisance—but to my buddy Pat, it had been quite a scare.

Anyone who flies for a long time will eventually run into these situations. All you can do is train to the best of your ability for emergencies. When something happens, keep your head cool and make the best possible decisions.

Huffman was not only bigger than Ambassador, but I had to admit that it was better run. The personnel were more professional and more enthusiastic, but the facilities cried out for development. My master plan was to make it a one-stop shop for aviation enthusiasts. I took every penny of profit from Huffman and reinvested it to that end. I refurbished the classrooms and bought flight simulators for both the one and the two engine planes we used with our students. I even built a restaurant that I called the Cockpit Café so my personnel had a nice place to have lunch and visiting pilots could grab a bite to eat.

The Cockpit Café also served as a place to reward loyal customers. When my pilots bought a certain number of gallons of fuel at my pump, they got a five-dollar coupon that they could use at the Cockpit Café. The only meal you could get for those five dollars was a hamburger, but hey, that was everybody's favorite meal anyway. Anybody doing the math could see that it was not worth flying a few miles extra to my airport to fuel at my tanks to get that free hamburger, but it worked. People loved feeling like their business was appreciated.

Huffman did indeed start to grow rapidly and in a very short time we had five times as many students than at Ambassador. Because of the accreditation, which could give college credit for American students, I acquired more students from the United States, while the student population at Ambassador was one hundred percent foreigners. The tremendous growth meant that I had to work very hard, but I loved every minute of it.

Meanwhile, a third aviation business opportunity presented itself to me. Business people from Naples often had to go to meetings in Florida's big cities such as Miami or Tallahassee, where the Florida legislative body meets. Because of the huge distances, cars are too slow and public transportation in Florida—and really, the entire United States—is essentially nonexistent. This meant there was a need for a charter service. It took me about a year of planning to put Ambassador Charter together. It functioned like an air-taxi service. It did the job, but it was an expensive option. To my mind, Florida needed a dependable, affordable, and regularly scheduled commuter service. The very thought made my heart race and I daydreamed about a fleet of small planes with one or two flights back and forth between Orlando, Fort Lauderdale, Jacksonville, and all of the other cities in Florida where business was flourishing. I thought that maybe Wally's money could make my dream a reality.

Wally thought it was a great plan, but he objected to the idea of "small planes." He thought we needed jet planes so we would look like a true airline. I certainly didn't object, and I started to make my calculations, looking for airplanes, think about marketing plans, and keeping an eye out for future personnel. This business plan for Florida Air, which we would abbreviate on the planes themselves to "Flair," was five years in the making and was finished just before 2000. We found nineteen-passenger Jetstream J 31 planes, a British airplane, which had proven itself both in Europe and America. We ordered six of them, hired personnel, and the business was ready to go. To my huge disappointment, I had to abide by the rules of the Federal Aviation Administration, specifically the DOT (Department of Transportation), which stipulated that I was not allowed to own more than one quarter of the airline. That meant that Wally and I each owned 24.9 percent. The remaining fifty percent was in the hands of a group of investors under the leadership of Ron Weyers, Wally's former partner in the insurance business.

 I was working like a maniac. Even though I owned less than a quarter of the company, I was the only active member and the working CEO. I bought a recently bankrupt airline for three-quarters of a million dollars, so I could use their paperwork, which would allow me to operate an airline. The next step was tackling the paperwork with the DOT. The moment you put your request in their hand, you are completely dependent on them. One of their demands is a financial fitness test, which requires proof that you can run for three months without any income. It is an incredibly demanding test, because for three months you have to pay pilots, landing rights fees, fuel, office personnel, etc. All that money is going out and not a penny is coming in.

I called my Washington, DC aviation lawyer John Gullick and asked if it might be a good idea to get some political support for the plan. He agreed so I sent a batch of letters to members of Congress, Florida politicians, and any other hotshots I thought might support Florida's first airline. I was universally supported by the Florida Minister of Finance, Katherine Harris, Governor Jeb Bush, and the Democratic senators Bob Graham and Bill Nelson. All of them sent letters of support in the first few months of 2001 to Norman Y. Mineta, the United States Secretary of Transportation.

Unfortunately, sometimes you can be too enthusiastic and things can backfire. This is what happened in our case, resulting in the DOT process grinding to a halt. The political pressure we deployed annoyed them, and after three months, we still had not heard a word. A year after our initial application, I was sitting with ambitious plans and huge costs, but no permission to start Florida Air. We had invested five million dollars, but we hadn't earned a penny.

The media caught on to our plans and the headline "Aviator Flies High with New Service" appeared in The Business Journal of Tampa Bay on January 22, 2001. They interviewed me at length about everything from the desirability of a commuter service to the symbolic meanings of the colors we used. I had painted the jet planes very deliberately. For me, Florida is all about the beautiful ocean and sky, and my planes were dark blue for the ocean at the bottom and light blue on top for the sky. The very top and the tail was sunflower yellow, indicating both the beautiful sun of Florida and to honor the original owners of the planes, Sunrise Air. They were the first brightly painted airplanes in Florida. In 2000, this was still a novelty, but I thought it was as "Florida" as you could get. "There are people who say it's ugly, but you remember it," I told the interviewer. "It's a marketing device; it's Florida, and it's fun. What's wrong with that?"

The reaction to all our publicity ranged from wildly enthusiastic to merely positive. Only the Venice Gondolier Sun, the local paper, didn't like my way of doing business. Even though my students put an enormous amount of money into the local economy and I employed many locals, if I was late with my rent it became headline news. In the period before 9/11 that was the only exciting news headlines Venice, Florida had.

One way or another, I had to get my airline up and running. I would not give up until I found the legal loophole that would allow me to move forward. I found it in Seattle, Washington, the state known for its rainy summers and snowy winters. Rick Boekle owned Harbor Air, a commuter service there that he ran with a bunch of Cessna Caravans. He was doing what we wanted to do in Florida, but his problem was that he had no business in the cold winter months. In Florida, the winter months are our high season, just the opposite of his situation. Harbor Air had all the correct FAA papers and was in desperate need of work in the winter. My solution was to have Harbor

Airlines fly the routes for us while Florida Air was waiting for the paperwork. The only thing we had to do was tell the DOT that Harbor Air was now flying a commuter service in Florida. Legally, they just had to announce their intention; there were no additional permissions necessary. We made the arrangements and I started to advertise, making sure that I always properly announced that Florida Air was temporarily in the hands of Harbor Air. Now the airline was up and running and what a glorious thing it was. My pilots were trained on Rick's airplanes and flew between Sarasota, Tallahassee, Fort Myers, and Key West, our first routes. The only problem with the Cessna Caravans was that they only transported nine passengers, but at least we were in business. Even more remarkable was that we were sold out from the very first day. The summer of 2001 certainly had its challenges, but things were happening. The airline was up and running, Ambassador had just had its first profitable year, and after all my work Huffman, had more than met my expectation—we had doubled the business.

My instinct, that little voice in my head, continued to protect me in the aviation business. In 1997, a man named Amos Watson from Marco Island was one of my customers. I had a Beechcraft King Air A-90 airplane that he really liked and he also asked me to find a King Air for him, too. It's not easy to find a good one, but after searching for two months, I found one that seemed perfect. I called the sellers, talked to them, and everything sounded great. Then I called Amos and told him I had found a plane. We flew to Texas with a commercial airline on a one-way ticket because we thought he'd buy the plane and we'd fly it back. I called the insurance company, told them what we were doing, and set up the insurance to cover us in case we bought it.

We flew to southwest Texas. When we arrived, the people selling the plane were standing outside the hangar. They were really warm and friendly, so we talked for a little while. But before I even saw the plane for the first time, I had a bad feeling. My gut told me not to fly the plane, the same sort of feeling I'd had before that flight to Switzerland. I did not feel comfortable telling Amos about my gut feeling, so I was planning to look for something in the logbooks to use as an excuse to back out of the sale. I had to find something; there was no way I going to let him buy this plane. I looked carefully at the logbooks, but I could not find anything—it all looked perfect. We went out to lunch and had a great time with these extremely pleasant and gracious people. The nicer they were, the worse I felt, because I did not want to fly that plane. After lunch, Amos was excited about the whole deal and ready to fly the plane.

I took Amos aside and said, "I need to talk to you."

He said, "Sure, go ahead, talk."

I told him, "Not here. Outside." Once we were outside, I said, "Amos, I advise you not to buy that plane. The books are perfect, everything is great, but it doesn't feel right. I don't pretend to understand, but do not do this."

Amos looked at me and asked, "Why?" in five different ways, but all I could say was, "I have a bad feeling. If you buy it, I am not going with you. I will fly back on a commercial plane."

He was furious with me, but said, "I guess if I pay you to give me advice, I have to take it. You tell these people the bad news; I'm staying out of this."

I went to the seller and said, "Sir, we are not buying the plane." They were surprised and asked why not. I just said, "We changed our minds," because I couldn't tell them my feelings.

The man shrugged and said, "No problem; I have other people lined up."

They were very considerate sellers and returned our deposit. A few weeks later, I found another plane for Amos and I put the incident out of my mind. Three or four months later, Summer, the secretary at my flight school in Naples, received a phone call from an insurance company.

The girl from the insurance company said, "I'm so very sorry about your boss. It was such a terrible thing to have happened."

My secretary asked, "What do you mean?"

"Well," she said. "He had that accident and was killed. We are terribly sorry."

Summer replied, "He's sitting here next to me, right now, alive and well!"

The girl from the insurance company was confused and asked, "Am I calling the right people? Weren't you the folks with the King Air that went down?"

Summer told her, "You have the wrong people, but why don't you fax us the information about the crash?"

They sent a news article in which I learned that the people who were selling the King Air did meet with other buyers that same day I was there with Amos. Those buyers took the plane for a test flight and it crashed, killing all aboard. Apparently the original engines had been replaced, but they forgot to fix the prop reverse on both engines. When you land a turboprop like the King Air, you change the blades of the prop, which push the plane back so you can land in a shorter space. The stop pitch of the propeller reverse was not correct, so when they took off, the blades went in reverse. The wings broke off the body of the plane and the airplane fell out of the air.

After I told Amos about what happened, he asked me, "Was that what you felt?" I told him that I could not know for sure, but that must have been it. Amos was a good man and became a very good friend of mine. Later, when I had to sell off my company, he bought my hangar and helped me out in many other ways. He died a few years later from a heart attack and I still miss him.

It was the middle of 2001 and I was living the classic American dream. I was a poor boy from a terrible background who immigrated to America, worked hard for everything he had, and became a success. My plan was to grow my businesses for another couple of years, then slowly wind down and retire. Things were great and I wasn't even forty-five.

9/11

The summer of 2001 was busy, just the way I like it. Every day I was surrounded by the students who took classes in my schools. There were tons of plane rentals and the repair shop was a fabulous business. Florida Air was a huge success; every day more passengers wanted to use our service. I had excellent managers taking care of all the details and I was focused on getting Florida Air up and running before the Harbor Air planes had to go back to Seattle for their summer season.

    A nasty crisis occurred when the pilots told me they would no longer fly because they were not being paid. This was news to me, since I was paying Harbor a lot of money, and had no idea they were not receiving their paychecks. Then I found out that Harbor Airlines was in financial trouble, and was using its earnings from me to pay down debts rather than payroll. Additionally, the company had been threatened by the DOT with losing its license. I had no idea what their legal basis could have been, but they told Rick that if he continued to fly in Florida they would shut down his airline. Rick felt he had no choice and withdrew his pilots and licensing. In a single day, Florida Air had to shut down. I assured everybody that it was a temporary glitch. I was absolutely sure that we had passed the three-month test and our paperwork would be approved any day.

My confidence eroded as I began to realize that the DOT had no intention of ever cooperating. They were determined to destroy Florida Air. I wrote official letters asking the DOT for an explanation. I tried to clear up any misunderstandings that might have happened. I tried to hurry the process in any way possible. I was frantically busy trying to rescue my airline.

That is where I found myself on the eleventh of September: on the phone with a lady at the FAA in Washington, DC. I can't remember what aspect of Florida Air we were discussing, but she suddenly screamed into the phone, "Oh my god! A plane just crashed into the World Trade Center!"

I could not believe my ears and said to her, "What kind of a joke is that?"

"No, it's really true!" she said. "Somebody really flew into the World Trade Center."

I still did not believe her, and she got angry with me. "Well fine, don't believe me. Have a nice day," she snapped and hung up on me.

I walked out of my office into the central hall at Ambassador and called over a couple of the guys. I directed a few of them to get a television from one of the classrooms and place it in our lounge. Shortly, a group of fifteen of us were standing around, looking at the TV. It wasn't necessary to find a channel; every channel carried the exact same images.

None of us experienced aviators could explain how something as absurd as that could have happened. All of us who fly have experienced times when things go wrong in the air. The first time your motor quits on you, you are in a panic. Later on, you learn how to control your emotions. You learn step-by-step responses to get yourself out of these emergency situations. Sometimes your first set of actions does not produce a result, and the suppressed panic mounts. If you have been well trained, you now switch and begin the second set of procedures. Your heart races, your breathing comes more quickly, but you stay with the program and perform the maneuvers you have been taught. All of us who fly know this feeling, and our hearts went out to the pilot who must have gone through procedure after procedure trying to avoid this gigantic catastrophe. There must've been a moment when he realized that nothing he was doing was going to avert this disaster. At some point, he must've realized he was going to die and that many people would die with him. Who knows what last prayers he might have said, what last images of loved ones might have flashed before his eyes. Our eyes were glued to that little screen, and everybody was silent.

The moment we got used to that first shock, we saw the second Boeing. We watched the plane make an unimaginable maneuver. The pilot went into a very steep turn.

Somebody in the group cried out, "What the hell is he doing?"

After the first plane hit one of the towers, a huge portion of the world must have turned on their TVs.

Bad news travels fast. I'm certain that a huge number of people around the world saw that second plane hit the towers live, as it happened, just like we did. We all realized at the same moment that a second plane proved this was not an accident. This was coordinated action. This was terrorism.

As we watched that second Boeing go into its turn, I hoped for just a moment that the pilot would miss its target. I hoped he would fly past the tower. I didn't have time to think what his next action might be. At the time, I also did not realize that the pilot created a forty-degree turn as a panicked maneuver to hit his goal. Afterward, one of us said that it was the move of an inexperienced pilot. Somebody with a lot of experience does not have to make such a steep turn to make something happen, and certainly not at full speed. What that meant to us was that the pilots of both airplanes were dead long before their planes crashed into the buildings. These had to be rookies behind the controls, even though they had managed to hit their goal.

Many of us have looked death in the eye at some point in our lives, some of us multiple times. We have all lost friends to carelessness, stupid accidents, and deadly coincidence. Most of us standing in that room had some life experience and it had toughened us up. This was something entirely different. We stood around and stared at the screen, unable to do anything.

The television would stay on the entire day; we kept ourselves informed as the tragedy developed in front of our eyes. We watched people jump to their deaths. To our absolute amazement, we watched the South Tower collapse into a perfect heap, as if demolition technicians had taken their time setting the appropriate charges. Exactly half an hour later, the North Tower collapsed in the same way, imploding rather than toppling over. All of us will remember that horrible day as disaster piled on top of disaster. During the morning, we heard of other attacks, about other hijacked planes on their way to unknown targets in America. By that time, I had already sent my pilots back to their hotels. Once I realized this was terrorism, I signaled the few pilots that were already in the air and ordered them to land. I called Huffman Aviation and told them to do the same thing. I ordered all of my planes grounded before the FAA got around to it. I remembered seeing the news the night before and realized that President Bush was in Sarasota. On my own initiative, I called the tower at Venice Airport and told them to close down the airport. The person whom I talked to did not think that was necessary. It seemed logical to me that you would do your utmost to protect the President of the United States, and that particular objective trumped some little rule that governed ordinary situations. However, that particular gentleman did not believe in being proactive and was content to wait for the FAA to make the decision for him. All this took place before the North Tower collapsed.

The repair people went back to their work for a bit to steady their nerves. During lunch, we talked over the news, and we all agreed we would not fly that entire day and maybe not even the next. We knew this would be a huge setback for the aviation industry in general and also for us personally. But the cost being paid by those who were affected in New York was unimaginably bigger. It was the general consensus that it would have been an even bigger disaster if the planes had missed their target and had crashed in the middle of New York City. It was a cynical conclusion, but we all had to agree.

We were hungry for facts. We wanted to know how badly the Pentagon had been hit, if the White House had been a target, or if the Capitol would collapse like the towers. There was sadness and anxiety, and nobody was in their right mind. I certainly couldn't work any longer and spent all my time watching television. As the evening wore on, it was finally clear that four airplanes had been hijacked and that all four were destroyed. American Airlines flight 11 flew into the South Tower of the World Trade Center, United Airlines flight 175 flew into the North Tower of the Trade Center, United Airlines flight 93 crashed in a meadow in Pennsylvania, presumably on its way to the Capitol in Washington, DC, and American Airlines flight 77 had flown into the Pentagon. It was unclear how many people had died. There was no doubt that all the passengers in the planes had met their deaths in those crashes.

In addition to the two towers, building number seven in Manhattan, which was forty-seven stories high, had collapsed because of the attack. Ground Zero was overflowing with rescue workers and firefighters desperately looking for survivors. I had never seen the proud, hard-working, and almost always optimistic Americans so confused. They had all been touched and their hearts were broken. I sat in front of the TV set looking at the facts, listening to theories of what might have happened, and absorbing the misery until late in the evening.

9/12 PART 1

The next day, September twelfth, I was awakened at half-past six by my office manager, Susan Desantis. After the exhausting events of the previous day, I had fallen into an extremely deep sleep, and it was difficult to come to full consciousness. Susan had never called me out of bed. Actually, I had never been called by anybody in my business at this hour, so when I heard her voice on the phone, I knew immediately that something was very wrong.

After the attacks of the previous day, the FAA had stopped all flights in the United States, and flights underway to the US had to land in Canada instead. All smaller airplanes had to land as quickly as possible, and no flights were allowed to leave. In other words, the entire airspace was empty. That was the second reason why I knew that Susan had no reason to be at the office, and certainly no reason I could think of to call me at that hour.

The news she gave me was even more devastating than I could have imagined in my darkest moments. Susan offered her apologies for calling me at this early hour, but she herself had been called out of bed at half-past two by the chief investigator at the FBI, Kelly J. Thomas. He had told her that the FBI had found an abandoned rental car at Logan Airport, the main airport at Boston, which contained Huffman Aviation brochures. The car had been rented by the pilots who crashed the two planes into the World Trade Center. They were two men who we knew very well: our former pupils Mohammed Atta and Marwan al-Shehhi. Atta was the pilot who had flown into the first World Trade Center tower and Shehhi had flown into the second tower.

I could not believe what I was hearing. This had to be a nightmare. I asked Susan to repeat the message and she calmly repeated the information. She understood how difficult it was for me to comprehend this. She told me that the FBI man had called Dale Krausse, the former general manager at Huffman, to get the files on Atta and Shehhi. Dale had not worked for Huffman Aviation for a while, and he had given Susan's number to the FBI. She had driven to the office and opened the door for two FBI agents. Together with those men, she looked for the relevant documents. The FBI agents had not considered it necessary to call me, and Susan had decided to allow me some extra sleep. But they had not been able to find the documents they needed, and Susan had called me. At my request, she put the senior man, Mr. Thomas, on the phone. He was very accommodating and friendly, and explained to me that they needed the files on those two ex-pupils.

"Shouldn't I be there?" I asked him.

"No, sir, that is not necessary. But if you know where those two files would be..."

I promised them that I would be there as quickly as possible so I could to talk to them in person. Of course I remembered Atta and Shehhi.

DEAD MAN WALKING

It was a beautiful summer day, the first day of July in a brand new century. The sky was blue, and the sun repeated its near-perfect daily performance here in Florida. I was expecting a busy day as usual. It was a coincidence that I found myself speaking with a coworker in the reception area of the main building of Huffman Aviation when two unremarkable-looking men walked in.

Their features were typical of people of the Middle East, but they wore standard American clothing: T-shirts, jeans, and sneakers, and looked like every other student at our flight school. About ten percent of our students came from the Middle East; there were no commercial flight schools there and the only way to learn how to fly was to be in the military. The two men looked around with the typical questioning look of customers in search of help. The shorter one was a lean man in his early thirties and at 5' 7", he was on the short side compared to most American men. He had a square face, dark hair, and brown eyes. He looked unfriendly and in a bad mood. The other one I thought was perhaps in his early twenties. My first impression was that he was a friendly bear of a man. He was slightly overweight; I would guess around 250 pounds, which was too much even for his tall 6' 2" frame. He looked pleasantly through a pair of metal rim glasses. It was obvious that the bear was the servant of the short man.

I knew I was right in that first impression the moment I walked up to them and asked if I could help with anything. The short one stuck out his hand and introduced himself as Mohammed Atta. The tall one followed his lead and told me his name was Marwan al-Shehhi. That was the last I heard out of his mouth for a while because Mohammed Atta did all the talking. They explained that they were aspiring pilots. They had taken classes in our neighborhood, with Jones Aviation in Sarasota, and they had some training on single engine airplanes. However, they did not like the school and were looking for a new place to study and complete their certification. They were definitely interested in commercial certification, he explained.

This is a slightly unusual situation because it is rare that students simply walk in off the street. Foreign students usually contact us via the Internet or in writing. Even though it was an unusual situation, their explanation made complete sense. I imagined that they had probably chosen their aviation school based on information they had received in their country, half a world away. Once they had gotten to Florida, the school had not met their expectations. It takes about half a year and a ton of money to get your license, and to spend all that time, money, concentration, effort, and energy at a place you don't like is no fun at all. It was not that hard to understand why they were looking for an alternative and why they had walked into our school, which was easy to find once they were in Florida.

High season in Florida is the winter. The temperature is moderate, and Florida is a haven for many people escaping the cold of the northern states. The summer is very warm and often humid, so that was always our slow season. To pick up two extra students in July was a bonus. Since it takes about half a year for a student to get a license, they would be leaving exactly as my busy season began, dumping an additional $40,000 into my business. No right-minded entrepreneur would lose an opportunity like that. It's not my job to greet and interview new potential students, and under ordinary circumstances, I would never have taken the time to give them a tour of our facilities. But when I saw their eager looks, I put on my winning smile and treated them to my best sales pitch.

I explained that Huffman Aviation was a part 141 school, ideally suited for foreign students. I told them what facilities we had, how much studying they would have to do, the sorts of planes we flew, and the high qualifications of our instructors. My story was equal parts hard information and glowing advertisement for my school. I was proud of my flight school and could honestly say that it was probably the best in our area.

As I interviewed them, it turned out that Atta already had his single engine license. He had flown forty hours, which could be subtracted from the 200 hours he needed for his commercial license. At that point, he could already fly solo. Shehhi had flown for ten hours and was not yet licensed, but he had gone on his first solo flight. At our school, students could expect to take their first solo flight after about ten to fifteen hours and could expect a single engine license after forty hours, so both men were on track. However, they still needed quite a few flight hours and theoretical training.

I asked them where they were from, and they told me without hesitation that they were from the United Arab Emirates. Much later, I found out that Shehhi was indeed from the UAE, but Atta was from Egypt. Atta had a perfectly valid and legal American driver's license issued by the state of Florida, which did state that his country of origin was Egypt, but I had no reason to look at it. I asked them about their visa status, and Atta told me he had a B-1 visa, a business visa, and Shehhi had a tourist visa. I knew that wasn't good enough, so I told them they would have to file the appropriate papers. As a 141 flight school, we had no problem in helping them apply for a student visa that would allow them to legally study at our school as soon as we submitted their papers.

Atta told me there was one problem they had to overcome if they were going to join my flight school: they needed a place to stay. We frequently made these kinds of accommodations, though we usually have a bit more advance notice. But by now, I had enough contacts and options that I knew we could arrange something for them, so I told them I could help on that front.

I spent perhaps an hour with them. During that time, I figured out that Atta was a cold fish, not someone with whom I was going to spend any social time. Then again, socializing with my students was not necessary. I was happy if I knew the faces and names of all my students. The fact that this prospective student wasn't pleasant was the least of my problems, and it had no further influence on my doing business with them.

Back in the main building, I introduced the two to Nicky Antini, my student coordinator. She gave them brochures and the appropriate forms, then explained the costs, payment program and other aspects of the school. Because Atta had more hours under his belt, his study would cost somewhat less than Shehhi's. If they were good students and applied themselves diligently, that could also result in some savings, but all together, they would have to count on spending about $40,000. That seemed fine to them.

From the time when I first saw them in the lobby, I never felt the need to change my first impression of them. Shehhi was a pleasant guy, in the way that big, heavyset men sometimes are. He always had time for a couple of words, and he had no problem joining the discussion with fellow students. His English was good enough that he could both tell a good joke and understand the punchline when someone else told one. His vocabulary was large enough so that it included X-rated words, and he enjoyed off-color jokes, too.

All that friendliness disappeared the moment Atta showed up. Shehhi would immediately clam up and let Atta do all the talking. When Atta walked out of a classroom, Shehhi would follow him quickly. In front of me, he called Atta his uncle.

Atta was arrogant and cold—basically a jerk. Mostly, he seemed like a spoiled child without any regard for others. Looking back, I realize this was because of his intense hatred and contempt for Americans and all non-Muslims. His mission forced him to interact with all sorts of people, in all sorts of situations, in a culture he despised and wanted to destroy. I now understand why he was in such a foul mood. His blank face and fixed eyes never changed. Because of that look, I called him "dead man walking," which, in retrospect, is a sick, if accurate, joke. Atta must have realized every day that he was working to complete a course that would ensure his death. I guess that could put a person in a bad mood.

They returned on the third day of July, and I happened to be there that day as well. They told us they had decided to come and study with us as long as I could find them a place to live. I left the two of them with Nicky to do their paperwork to apply to the school and for the appropriate visa, and I walked away to talk to my bookkeeper, who occasionally rented out rooms.

I considered our helpfulness with issues like the visa application and lodging as the kinds of services that set our school apart. Neither of these matters were our responsibility, but I saw offering our help as good marketing and good relationship-building. As far as the visa application was concerned, all we needed to do was send them to the INS. They could start training immediately because prior approval was not necessary. Most students did not get their actual visa until it was time to for them to leave.

Nicky, the staff person who dealt with these student issues, was not an experienced employee. At twenty-one, she was a little bit older than my oldest daughter. She was originally hired to wash airplanes at Huffman, but she quickly complained that the work was too physically demanding; out of pity, I had given her an office job. She was on probation as student coordinator when Atta and Shehhi arrived. Unfortunately, it turned out that office work was also too challenging for her. She made mistakes, including a mistake in the application for Atta and Shehhi that I found some months later. She did not fill out the I-20M forms until the twenty-ninth of August, an act I attribute to her laziness, and she also never properly signed their paperwork. But the government never noticed, and their applications were accepted without further comment.

My bookkeeper Charlie Voss told me that he had no problem renting out a room to the two Muslim guys. He just needed to ask his wife if it was all right with her. Their spare bedroom, which had two single beds, had been rented out to our students before for seventeen dollars per night. He called his wife and she agreed to take in the new students.

They did not show any gratitude for this favor. I didn't know it at the time because Charlie Voss never complained to me, but I eventually found out that they made a mess of their room and their bathroom. After they took a shower, it was apparently their custom to shake themselves dry like dogs, leaving water everywhere, instead of drying themselves with a towel. When Mrs. Voss complained, they yelled back at her, and after a few days, the atmosphere in the house deteriorated significantly. After a few more incidents in which Atta and Shehhi were very rude to Mrs. Voss, Charlie threw them out of his house and told them to find shelter elsewhere, which they did without a problem.

I saw them in our little kitchen just about every day. The kitchen was in the main building where there was a coffee maker and some vending machines for soda and snacks. That was one of the two places at Huffman where we all socialized, and it was a favorite spot for students to hang out between classes. Most students were far away from home and often more than a little bit homesick, which drove them to socialize with each other more than they might in other situations. That was not true for Atta and Shehhi. They were stand-offish, although they talked with two British students of Middle Eastern descent once in a while.

A few weeks after they came to Huffman, I started a conversation with them in the kitchen. I often tried to have some friendly contact with the students because it somewhat lightened the otherwise oppressively serious study atmosphere. I thought maybe these two were just feeling uncomfortable and maybe I could help them adjust a bit with some friendly banter.

"Hey Mohammed," I started, "you've got to tell me why you want to become a pilot."

He was immediately suspicious. "Why do you want to know?"

"I read your admission papers, and I saw that you studied architecture at the Technical University in Hamburg. That is quite an accomplishment. And it is a big change to suddenly become a pilot."

"I'm sick of architecture." he replied curtly.

Later I found out that his dissertation was on the rebuilding of ancient Arabic cities, particularly how to combine traditional Arab building methods with modern conveniences. As a motto for his dissertation, he chose a prophetic verse from the Quran, Sura six, verse 162. "Say: My Salat (the obligatory prayers that are performed by Muslims five times a day), my worship practices, my life, and my death, are all devoted absolutely to GOD alone, the Lord of the universe." However, there was no way for us to know how twisted his interpretation of this verse had become by the time he had come to our school.

"The aviation business is no picnic, either," I continued. "It used to be that a pilot could make good money, but those days are gone. Anyway, you are almost thirty-two years old. Shehhi is still a young guy, and he won't have any problem finding a job because he is only twenty-two, but things are different for you."

"It's not a problem," he replied. "We love to fly, and we both have good jobs waiting for us when we return to the United Arab Emirates. All we need is to get our license."

That seemed to be a good, watertight argument. It was not my intention to argue with them, anyway; I merely to attempt some casual conversation. I also wanted to establish enough of a relationship so I could ask them if they had some friends back home who might like to come and study with us. We could always use more students. The irony of my intentions is very clear to me now, but at the time, I was just a businessman trying to drum up more business.

As unfriendly as they were toward me, they were horribly rude and obnoxious to all of our women employees. We had seen this before with the young

Muslim students. Their behavior towards women was very different from that of young European and American men, but Atta crossed some well-defined boundaries. They did not threaten our women or behave as sexual predators, but they were utterly without respect for them.

After a couple of weeks, the first complaints started to come in. Atta had ordered breakfast at the Cockpit Café, a standard American breakfast of fried eggs, toast, and a cup of coffee. When the food arrived, he took one look at his food and dropped the entire plate, food and all, on the floor. I don't know if the service had been too slow, or if the eggs had been cold, but he simply got up and walked out without paying. The waitress had not seen any of this happen, but a fellow customer had witnessed the whole thing with open-mouthed astonishment. It was deliberate, a clear provocation, and a petty show of disrespect.

The worst of the complainants that finally did reach me came from my head pilot, Daniel Purcell. Daniel came to me to tell me about what was going on with Atta and Shehhi, which surprised me because discipline problems rarely reared their heads with the adult students. It was the pampered kids whose rich parents had not bothered to teach them manners who tended to act up once they were away from the immediate adult supervision that kept them in check in their home countries. I had occasionally been forced to send one of these spoiled brats packing. After all, we work with airplanes, which are expensive machines, and the objective is to fly, which is a dangerous occupation. In our profession, a sense of responsibility is not optional. But you expect something a little better from two grown men.

"Why? What are they doing?" I asked Daniel.

"They just don't listen; not to Mark and not to Thierry (their instructors). They are not serious about their studies, and in the plane they just mess around. They are not obeying the instructions they are given. They just ignore their instructors and act like a couple of teenagers," he said.

I was not particularly concerned about any dangerous situations that might develop. As long as they were flying with instructors, the situation would be kept under control. While such childish behavior was annoying, it was also potentially damaging to my school's reputation. When a student fails the FAA examinations, their instructor has to make a record of it. The FAA reviews all instructors every two years. Instructors who have failed more than the average number of students have to take extra classes and pass another exam. It is a bother and I have never met an instructor who did not find the procedure embarrassing. It is the equivalent of being called in by the principal to be told you are failing your classes and need to go to summer school.

I didn't like it for another reason. When rich parents enroll their children at my school, they need to be confident that my instructors can teach their children how to pass the FAA exams. Failing students was not a reputation I could afford. I told Daniel that he had my permission to throw them out if they would not behave, but he should first give them one more try. I told him to give them the riot act—emphasize that he had discussed this with me, and that we were in agreement. If they did not treat their instructors with more respect and show friendlier behavior to their colleagues and the personnel, Daniel had my personal permission to throw them out.

Two days later, I had a little talk with Atta and Shehhi myself. I wanted to make sure there was no misunderstanding and that they knew that Daniel had my complete trust and confidence. I repeated what Daniel must have told them, as well, namely that they had to obey instructions, and we would not tolerate them treating anybody in my facility with contempt.

Frankly, I had expected Atta to get furious with me. To my surprise, he said absolutely nothing. He did not explain, nor did he apologize. He simply looked at me with his customary angry stare and walked away. He might not have been responsive during our talk, but their behavior did change. My instructors no longer complained and I forgot about this minor incident.

The only one who continued to occasionally complain about Atta and Shehhi was Susan Desantis, my office manager. I chalked those complaints up under the 80/20 rule. If you analyze your business, you will find that 80 percent of your problems are caused by only 20 percent of your clients, whereas the other 80 percent of your clients only give you 20 percent of all the headaches. Susan's complaints made me aware that after their dressing down, these two had not morphed into sweet guys, but they seemed to make an effort to blend into the flight school after we confronted them.

They came to class and flew in the two-person Cessnas (152 and 150) and later in the Cessna 172.

They graduated to our Warriors and finally, to the Pied Piper Seneca. They had their meals and drank their coffee at the Cockpit Café and could be found in the classrooms studying theory and putting in their time on the flight simulator. They were just two ordinary students and none of the forty-eight people who worked at Huffman Aviation ever voiced a doubt about their true identity.

In fact, they did not stand out to us as fanatical, much less mildly serious Muslims. In contrast to many of our Muslim students, they never took advantage of the prayer mats we had provided for their religious duty of praying five times a day. They also did not obey the religious rule that forbids the eating of pork. They ate their hamburgers at the Cockpit Café just like everyone else, burgers that were cooked on the same grill on which the morning bacon and sausage were prepared. They never even asked if any of the food conformed to Halal standards. I know for a fact that Shehhi ate pork.

Years later, I learned why a radical Muslim could behave this way. The rules of Islam give a dispensation to those Muslims who devote their lives to the holy war, the Jihad. Because they are sacrificing themselves and serving a higher purpose, they are allowed to do the things forbidden to an ordinary Muslim, such as eat pork and drink alcohol.

After our last unpleasant encounter, I tried one more time to have a pleasant conversation with Atta. I saw him next to the coffee maker one day and suddenly remembered that he had studied in Germany. I thought that maybe he would enjoy hearing German again.

Germany shares part of its border with the Netherlands, and my education had included taking a few years of German language classes that were a standard part of the curriculum. Because I had done some business in Germany as well, I was fluent in the language.

"Guten Morgen, wie geht's?" I said to him. It is nothing more complicated than a standard "Good morning, how are things?" in German.

Well, he was surprised, all right—Atta looked as if he saw water burning! Of course, I did not know that he had been living for years with his secret mission, and that he was afraid that he might be stopped if anybody suspected him. His real employers must have pressed on his heart that he had to be very careful.

I can now imagine the panic that must have been running through his head when he suddenly heard me speak German. For a moment, he might have thought that he had been found out, that he had been followed from Germany, and that his big plan was about to come crashing down. He must also have been wondering if he had ever said something in German that he needed to keep secret, something I might have overheard and understood.

Of course, I had no idea about all that, though I was certainly surprised that he did not utter a single word in response to my greeting. Not in English, not in German, and not in any other language. He was silent for a moment, while his brain was no doubt working overtime to consider all the implications. After an awkward silence of ten seconds, he turned around and walked away. My attempt at friendship had failed, but it would take more than a year for me to find out why.

Shehhi, who was standing beside Atta at the time, did not walk away. We talked for a little while in English because he could not be seduced into speak in German, though he too must have been fluent. We talked about his upcoming job at the national airline of the United Arab Emirates. His "uncle" Atta would also work there. Little by little, I built up a picture of Shehhi's parents, who had sent their beloved son with his unpleasant uncle Mohammed to faraway Florida. I almost felt sorry for him. Without the immediate influence of Atta, Marwan was more cooperative, at least on a superficial level.

Atta often had problems starting the planes and frequently complained loudly about how badly our planes were maintained. The complainants were groundless because, without exception, it was always his fault. I don't know if it was because he didn't pay attention to detail or lacked patience, but even after he was licensed, Atta flooded the motor more often than most students did after two weeks of instruction.

Eventually they got their licenses. On the sixth of November, 2000, my instructor Thierry Leklou decided that Atta had enough theoretical knowledge to take the written IFR exam. On the twentieth of November 2000, he passed the IFR exam, and on December twenty-first, he passed his commercial-license examination, five months after beginning his course with us. He had flown more than 178 hours, 108 of them with an instructor, and had almost sixteen hours of theory classes. Shehhi got his private license on the ninth of December, 2000, took the IFR exam on November twentieth and got his commercial license on the same day as Atta. The FAA examiner Dave Whitman concurred that they were average pilots, and judged their flying good enough to pass them. Shehhi had flown more than 192 hours, 123 with an instructor and had taken twenty-two hours of theory classes.

At last, they were both ready to be commercial pilots. They could rent themselves out as aviation tour guides, they were allowed to transport parachutists and release them in the air, and other such activities, though they were limited to planes of 12,000 pounds. I assumed they would go back to their own country and continue their education.

Getting their licenses certainly didn't make them any less unpleasant. A couple of days later, Atta and Shehhi rented our Piper Warrior with the call letters N55SHA and flew to Miami International Airport. A couple of hours later, I got a call from a furious inspector at the FAA. He yelled at me that a student of mine by the name of Mohammed Atta had acted with complete lack of responsibility.

"He was formerly a student of mine," I explained, "But he is no longer one. He has his commercial license, so if there is a problem, it is his responsibility." That piece of information calmed the man down a bit.

"But are you the owner of the Piper Warrior N55SHA?"

"Yes, that is our plane. Is there anything wrong with it?"

The man told me that Atta and Shehhi had left the plane in the middle of the runway. I could not believe my ears. Miami International is a gigantic airport. It is a terrible decision to fly there with such a small airplane, and is a completely crazy thing for pilots with so little training to do. It is the equivalent of letting a kid who just got his driver's license drive in a NASCAR race. Furthermore, it is the height of unprofessional behavior to leave a plane on a runway. Minimally, it creates a life-threatening situation, and it is very understandable that the guys in Miami were furious.

Atta called me a short time later. He had the nerve to be angry with me because I had rented him a plane that "had not been properly maintained" and "would not work." He never even apologized for his own irresponsible behavior. Instead, he demanded that I pay his taxi fare back to Venice because it was my fault. I lit into him. I yelled at him, telling him that I had no intention whatsoever of paying for anything and that he had behaved with an astonishing lack of responsibility. I was sure that the technical problems had all been his fault and that he had flooded the motor as usual. He was quiet for a moment and then hung up the phone, robbing me of the opportunity to continue my rant.

Meanwhile, my plane was towed to one of the maintenance hangars. They investigated the problem and it turned out, just as I had predicted: he had flooded the motor. To be absolutely sure, the FAA requested the maintenance records for the plane and examined them under a microscope. They found no irregularities and, of course, when our pilot went to pick up the plane, he had no problem flying it back.

The day after their blunder, Atta and Shehhi were back. I showed Atta his bill and told him he had to pay up, and that I never wanted to see them on our field again. I didn't need the business of people who would treat my planes and the reputation of my flight school with such utter contempt. As usual, Atta looked furious and Shehhi remained polite.

This was the last time I saw the duo. They paid their bill in full on the fifth of January, 2001. I assumed that I would never hear anything more about Atta and Shehhi, and that was fine with me.

9/12 PART 2

I was still in bed, trying to get a grip on the situation. Susan and the FBI man reacted calmly and rationally to my words, so I must have sounded normal. Oddly enough, I needed that affirmation because I was confused. Maybe confused is not quite the right word. The moment Susan told me that Atta and Shehhi had flown into the World Trade Center, I left my body. I pride myself on being rational and calm, in control of my faculties even in situations of extreme stress, but I actually felt a part of myself float out of my body. I floated up to the ceiling, and I could see myself sitting at the edge of the bed with a phone in my hand. I have read about people who have that kind of experience when they die—for instance, on an operating table—and they float above the scene, watching the frantic surgeons bring them back to life. I was obviously very much alive at that moment, but my experience was just the same. I actually had to make a conscious effort to go back into my body.

I turned to Astrid and told her that the terrorists we watched destroy the World Trade Center towers were ex-students of ours. She also had a terrible shock, though she was never interested in my work. I had certainly never had occasion to tell her about these two, so she had no point of reference.

Her immediate reaction was, "Keep your mouth shut, don't tell anything to anybody, and certainly don't talk to journalists."

Her reaction did not surprise me in the least. In the United States, public opinion is very powerful, and you can easily become bad news. Astrid had no intention of being known as "that woman," the wife of the man who had some connection with the attacks on the World Trade Center. I could definitely understand her point of view, but it was also completely selfish. There was no way to hide my connection to the terrorists, it was much too big for that. I told this to her, got out of bed, dressed myself quickly, and drove full speed to Venice. If bad news hits your business, you, as the leader, need to take control immediately and make sure that the story is told accurately and completely.

The trip from Bonita Springs, which lies a little to the north of Naples, to the office at Huffman Aviation in Venice, is ordinarily a trip of an hour and a half. I did it in an hour. As I was driving, I got a call from Mr. Kelly, who said they had found the papers they needed and their suspicions were confirmed. Two of the people involved in the 9/11 attacks had indeed been students of mine. Since they had found what they wanted, he said I could turn around and go home. But, of course, I had no intention of staying away.

I assured them I was on my way and asked them to wait. A little while later, another FBI agent called me. He advised me not to talk to any journalists, but

I said that things would be much worse for me if I did not talk to them.

He repeated himself, "I advise you not to talk to any journalists."

"This is such a terrible thing," I told him, "I want to make sure that this story is told as accurately as possible. If I don't tell the story completely and fully, they will think I have something to hide." There was silence on the other side of the line. "Are you forbidding me?" I asked him, "Are you forbidding me to talk to the press?"

"What do you mean, Mr. Dekkers?"

"What I mean is, can you legally stop me from talking to journalists?"

"No, legally I can't do that, but I do advise you not to," he repeated.

"All right," I said to him, "Then I will tell you right now that I will talk to the journalists that come for the story."

Again he asked me why I intended to do that, and once again, I repeated my entire explanation. "Well then, all I can ask you is not to volunteer any details, just answer their questions," he said.

I promised him that I would do that. I never had to go back on the promise as I soon found out that the journalists had more information than I did. He also offered his help if I needed it. I thanked him for the offer and we hung up.

The closer I got to Venice, the more uncomfortable I became. I normally never leave my house until I move my bowels. This morning I had not taken the time for that necessary act, and it was now starting to bother me. I was using mind tricks to keep myself going and control the increasingly intense urge. Close to Venice, I saw a red light. Though I slowed down, I didn't stop and continued through the intersection after making certain it was clear. The only car in sight was one approaching from the distance. Unfortunately, that approaching car happened to be a police car. He stopped me and asked, "Why did you drive through the red light?"

I told him truthfully, "Because I really have to go to the bathroom, and I am in a lot of pain."

He was clearly not sympathetic to my plight. "Driver's license and registration, please."

I pleaded with him. "Officer, please. Follow me to my office, which is right around the corner. Please let me go to the bathroom first and after that, I will answer all your questions and pay for any penalties. I just don't want to shit in my pants!"

"Aren't you the guy from Huffman Aviation?" These days, that question doesn't surprise me at all, but at that moment, I was still an anonymous entrepreneur. From his reaction, I noticed that he already had been given a heads up. He was not willing to give me any leeway and continued to insist that I show him my license and registration.

I was fed up and said, "I'm going to the office. You can do as you please."

He immediately pulled out his gun and pointed it at me. "If you don't do what I say, I'll shoot you!"

I was so hyped up on adrenaline that I did not even register any shock. I just got angrier. "Jesus man, calm down. All I have to do is go take a dump. It's not a big deal."

He suddenly realized how absurd his overreaction was, and put away his gun. He made me promise I would never run another red light, got into his police car and drove away.

This bizarre incident taught me two things. First, I realized that from now on, I was a celebrity, and it didn't take much imagination to figure out whether I was going to be the good guy or the bad guy. Secondly, it seemed the events of the previous day had cost America a piece of her common sense. The moment I arrived at the office, I saw a few black cars, but I did not stop to take notice. I entered through the side door and ran to the bathroom, happy to have made it on time.

When I walked into the lobby, I found about six FBI agents waiting for me. With Susan's help, they had packed two boxes of papers, and they assured me again that my presence really was not necessary. Furthermore, they apologized for coming without the proper paperwork necessary to confiscate these documents. This was the first time anything like this had happened to me, and I told them they could take whatever they needed. In subsequent years, I have learned a bit about the huge legal ramifications of such an action on the part of law enforcement. At the time, any legal issues were the last thing on my mind. As far as I was concerned, we were at war, and I would behave like a true patriot. It did not matter to me that I was not an official American citizen; I knew where my loyalty and my heart were.

I offered them a great deal more material than they had initially come for. I grabbed every folder of every

Muslim student who had enrolled in the last couple of years at Huffman. They were a little surprised, but gratefully accepted what I gave them. Since they were at the very beginning of their investigation, they didn't really know what they were looking for, so it made sense to me to give them all the material that could possibly be relevant.

I told them that Atta and Shehhi had used our computers, and I offered to give them the hard drives to take with them. To my surprise, they were not enthusiastic about the idea, but I insisted and they finally accepted them. Later on, it would turn out that the computers contained crucial material. The FBI found information on my hard drives that eventually led them to the Hamburg terrorist cell, saving them weeks of painful investigation.

Weeks later, the FBI agents said that they could not tell me anything about the information they had gleaned from my papers, but they assured me that I did not have anything to fear about any of my other previous students. It was an enormous relief, and three months later they even returned my materials. It took more than a year for the FBI to let me know how useful my computers had been. Apparently, they had taken that long to get over the embarrassment of those six agents getting the computer hard drives only because I forced them to take them. I had behaved like a responsible citizen and it was a shame that their acknowledgment had taken so long.

The first journalists arrived before the FBI even left. Amy Oshier from the local Fort Myers NBC station was the first in what would become an endless parade.

As a resident of Florida, she happened to be in the perfect location, but it was her keen journalistic mind that allowed her to realize where the story would be.

She later told me that she grew up in the small town of Melbourne, Florida. "We had a flight school nearby and there were always students in our neighborhood from the Middle East. Some of these children attended my school while their fathers learned how to fly a plane. These sorts of people stand out like a sore thumb in Florida," she said. When she learned some of the terrorists had lived in Venice, she immediately realized that attending flight school was the only reason they would have been there. Once she put the pieces together, Amy drove around with her cameraman looking for the right airport in Venice. When she saw black SUVs in front of our office, she knew that she had hit the bull's-eye. Six black SUVs in one place could only mean one thing: FBI agents. She also told me that an interview for a news story doesn't usually last more than ten to fifteen minutes. However, she talked with me for an hour and a half that day. For me, it was a taste of things to come. For her, it was the beginning of a journalistic track that would later land her the Edward L. Murrow award, one of the most prestigious journalistic awards in this country.

After Amy left, I talked to my personnel. They were waiting for me because as long as there were no planes they could fly, there wasn't much to do around the office. When I told them about our connection with the 9/11 attacks, people were terribly upset. Some girls ran to the bathroom to throw up, others quit their jobs right then and there. The idea that they would continue to work in a place that had temporarily been home to these terrorists was unbearable to them. Meanwhile, a dozen or so trucks had parked in front of our office, all of them filled with journalists who wanted to get the story. I told my personnel that I would be the only one to talk to the press. My reasons were simple. The story that we told had to be consistent; I did not want to encourage confusing or contradictory stories. If any of them had anything they thought might be important, I told them to come to me or go to the FBI, but not to go to the press.

The mayhem and confusion that followed is hard to describe. Microphones were pushed in my face, cameras followed me everywhere, flashbulbs went off, and the questions did not stop. I must have given 150 to 200 interviews that very first day alone. I hardly had time to go to the bathroom again.

My world came to a complete standstill. The flight school could no longer function, so I did nothing but talk all day long. I had no idea what else was going on in the world. My only news came from the journalists with whom I was talking. They explained that the entire country was in mourning and that rescue workers in New York were still looking for survivors. I was told that the stock market was closed and that Osama bin Laden was the evil genius behind the plot.

My brain was working overtime. I wanted absolute transparency and for everyone to know that my school, my personnel, and I were innocent. I hoped that the media attention would dissipate quickly that way.

How could I have been so naïve? After the first

day, after the first couple of hours, I fell into hopeless repetition because there was simply nothing new or different to add. Years later, the journalists still come and ask the very same questions. Within a few weeks, my photograph made the front page of all the newspapers, and there wasn't a talk show program that didn't invite me. Larry King, CNN, Oprah—they all wanted interviews. National and international radio stations called me and asked for commentary. I could not really understand it. After all, I did not have any news. I had told my story over and over again, but had no time to wonder at the attention given to me.

There were four terrorists that flew the four planes, so journalists had gone to lots of flight schools in the United States where the terrorists had taken classes. All the other flight school owners, who undoubtedly had something to say, kept silent. Even my next-door neighbor at the airport of Venice, Arne Kruithof, had instructed the third terrorist. But Arne would not talk. Not until much later did I understand that the other flight school owners were scared that they would be seen as guilty. The strategy they employed was the exact opposite of what I did, and they ended up in a better situation because they kept quiet. However, all of us went bankrupt because we were considered guilty by association.

JOURNALISTS, THE NEWS, AND ME

When you've been in business for a while, you're bound to eventually make it into the news. Most businesses look for positive ways to become newsworthy because it's great marketing. Businesses don't sponsor Little League baseball teams or get involved with charities only out of the goodness of their hearts. In return for their support, they get to place their logos everywhere. It's an accepted part of business and it benefits everybody. Some business people also end up in the news because they do something that media thinks will make a good story. Before 9/11, I had been interviewed for two major stories, neither of which I created intentionally.

My real first experience with the media was in 1995. At my flight school Ambassador Airways, we had completely overhauled a Cessna 152, a small two-seater airplane. It was painted a pretty blue and white, and it had a new engine and a completely new interior. I made the first flight in that rebuilt plane alone because I wanted to test her thoroughly, making sure she was safe before she went into the flight school. I decided to make a quick roundtrip from Naples to Orlando to pick up a private package I needed to get anyway. I was almost home in Naples, right above route 41 at Bonita Springs, when I heard my engine start to sputter. I looked at the fuel gauge and saw I still had fuel. I performed a cockpit check, making sure that none of the other indicators were off, and found that everything was fine. But my motor was about to give out and I had to land quickly. Route 41 was not as busy as it is now, but there were still electrical cables strung across the road. Thank goodness landing is one of my strengths. I flew under an electricity cable and landed the plane right between the driving cars. I promise there were some very startled drivers on the road that day.

About fifteen minutes later, the first TV truck arrived with their cameras. They all wanted to know what had happened, and I told them that I thought the carburetor had iced up because I still had fuel. I proved that point in front of the camera several times by letting some fuel spill out. When the sheriff came, I told him my engine sputtered and I had to land. I also told him that a colleague was coming to help me check the engine and would bring extra fuel. The sheriff asked why I needed that, and I explained that when you start a plane, it takes three to four times more fuel than normal flight at cruising speed. The sheriff told me I had to stay there, and he left the scene.

When my colleague arrived, we saw that there was no ice left on the carburetor because it had melted while I was waiting in the warm Florida weather. I put a little extra fuel in the plane and she was good to go. By now, it was almost three in the afternoon and traffic was starting to pick up. I really needed to leave immediately if I was going to fly the plane out safely. I called the sheriff's office and asked what I should do. The person on the phone began to explain that he had called the FAA, and I quickly said, "Good, thank you. Goodbye," and hung up the phone. I did not intend to give him the chance to tell me that the FAA wanted me grounded, because once he told me that I couldn't leave. Technically, he never told me and all I knew was that he had talked with the FAA. I quickly climbed into my plane, told my partner to block off the road, started the engine, and took off with no problem.

Back in the office at the Naples Airport, I talked with the an investigator from the FAA who asked me what happened. I told them I was cruising along and everything was fine, but suddenly the engine started sputtering, and I thought the carburetor might have iced up. The FAA investigator asked if I had put my carburetor heater on. He was right; I had indeed forgotten to do that. He was a great guy and said, "Yeah, that's what you had; you had ice. It's no problem, no harm done," and he let the matter drop.

The other time I had some contact with the media was in February of 1999, and it concerned a very upsetting incident. I had a customer named Mitchell Johnson, a big, tall, forty-seven-year-old single guy who loved to go to Key West. He was a new pilot, with ninety hours of flying time under his belt, and he rented planes from me and a few other places. I had a Cessna 210 N6174F that he really wanted to fly but I wouldn't rent it to him. Not only did he not have enough hours of flying time, but his level of experience did not give him the qualifications he needed for my insurance company to cover him. I had explained that to him clearly and he understood the issues involved.

The local airplane charter companies had an arrangement whereby we rented each other's planes if we had a customer who wanted something we did not own. I did not know this, but Mitchell had gone to Wolf Arrow Flying Club, another charter company, and requested a Cessna 210. They rented the plane from me, and were required by regulation to make sure their customer met my insurance company's requirements. However, they did not check him out thoroughly enough, and without my knowledge, they rented my plane to him. Mitchell was flying back from Key West on February fifth, approaching Naples airport a couple of minutes before ten at night, right before the control tower was closing. He was in a hurry because he wanted to land in Naples before the tower closed, but somebody else was landing ahead of him. The tower advised him to do a full 360, a "holding pattern," and told him he would be the next to land.

We will never know exactly what happened that night. He was an inexperienced pilot, night was falling, and maybe he was tired from a fun-filled weekend in Key West. All we know is that he turned the plane and flew into the Gulf at full speed. He hit the water so hard that he broke his safety belt and went through the front windshield. He was cut diagonally in two, from his hip to his neck, by one of the window styles.

His parents called me right after the accident, before

they knew what happened, and said, "Tell us what happened to our son. We only know that they took him out of the Gulf of Mexico."

I said, "Please don't ask me exactly what happened."

They said, "We understand that, but can you tell us if he survived?"

Nobody had told them the truth yet; the police would not confirm his death because they had to examine him first. I said, "Ma'am, I can't tell you anything specific, but one thing is for sure: he did not survive."

They answered, "Thank you for being honest; nobody wanted to tell us anything. We just needed to know." It was such a terribly sad moment, and my heart went out to those poor people. When they examined him later, they found no drugs in his system, so we do know that was not the problem.

We got the plane back, but it was completely destroyed. After the accident, the NTSB (National Transportation Safety Board, the independent Federal agency charged by Congress with the investigation of every civil aviation accident that includes a fatality) sent Corky Smith to investigate. In the beginning, he was very skeptical. He was a difficult man to get along with. He did an extremely thorough investigation of the plane and everything associated with it. He checked out the motor and found that it was in fine working order, even after the impact and being in the water. He looked very carefully at our maintenance records for the plane. After about four days, his behavior changed because he became convinced it was not our fault. Corky ended up becoming an acquaintance of mine, and we worked together a few times. He is a very nice guy and an extremely thorough professional when it comes to his work.

In the meantime, I had lost my plane, and the insurance company refused to pay me the $60,000 because the pilot did not have the right qualifications. Mitchell had insurance through Avoca in Orlando, FL, with a policy value of $45,000. This money was going to his parents, as Mitchell was single and had no other heirs. I decided not to sue the insurance company because I knew they would turn around and sue the parents, and the loss of their son was bad enough. It was a lot of money to lose, but back then, I could handle it and wanted to spare his parents.

Of course, the media talked to me about this accident and my highway landing, but those interviews had no effect on my business or me. The media circus around me after 9/11 has been of a different order of intensity for which I was not prepared. On September twelfth, I knew that the media would come around, and I expected to be answering questions for days. What I did not foresee is that I would be giving hundreds of interviews to reporters from all over the world during the next five years.

During the first couple of interviews on September twelfth, I used some strong language concerning the two men. I called Atta an asshole. When I talked about them both, I called them animals that I would have gladly murdered with my bare hands if I had known what they were up to. The entire incident immediately colored me as an anti-Muslim. I made these comments on camera and I was quite clear that I would never accept Muslims at my flight school again. I did apologize to the Muslim students in my school, explaining that it was not a personal attack against them. I can still barely talk about the events of 9/11 without getting emotional. The thought that I'd made it easy, even pleasant, for those two to take lessons, and the idea that I had given them the slightest degree of assistance in their horrible plans is still unbearable.

But to be fair, these interviewers had no idea what a raw nerve they had hit. This was not the first time my life had been impacted by terrorists.

During the last part of my high school career, my parents moved to Spain. A few years later, I decided to visit them in the Spanish town of Alicante. I was feeling good because I was doing well in my business, and Astrid and I were getting serious, so I wanted to introduce her to my parents. It was a wonderful vacation. Astrid and I loved the tropical warm weather. I had always loved warm weather, the warmer the better, and for Astrid, who comes from an Indonesian background, it was a return to her ancestral climate.

The reunion with my family was even more important to me. My father had made some changes in his life and now had a steady job. He was working for a Dutch company that helped people like himself move from Holland to Spain, a move as common in Holland as the flow of retirees to Florida in the United States. He was working in a warehouse that temporarily stored household goods for Dutch people while their Spanish homes were prepared.

My father took the initiative to straighten out the strained relationship between us. I had a long talk with him and he acknowledged that he had been much too tough on me in my youth and had treated me badly. He even apologized. It was an unbelievably emotional moment for me; I could barely hold back my tears. Though there was no way of making up for all of those years, my heart was at peace. My mother had also been kinder than I had ever experienced before during that long summer vacation. I was feeling great when Astrid and I drove back to Holland.

A few days later, the telephone rang and one of my aunts said, "Rudi, my boy, something terrible has happened in Spain. It is about your father."

"My father? What happened? Is he ill?"

"No, that's not it. He had a terrible accident, and it doesn't look very good," she said.

She could not give me any details, but the message was clear: I had to get there with all possible speed. It was a bitter moment. Just as I felt that I had finally been granted my rightful place in my family, this crisis happened that could take it all away. We packed our car and drove the 1,500 kilometers back to Spain.

We found my father in a coma at the hospital. He looked pale and thin, and had already lost a great deal of weight. The circumstances at the hospital were even more shocking than his condition. The hospital was not what I was used to in the Netherlands: a quiet place with antiseptic, tiled halls, and white walls where you could find the occasional quiet visitor and concerned nurses walking around. It seemed that in Spain, you were in the hospital for your medical procedures, but all of the rest of your care had to be provided by the family. This meant that loud, large, extended families were camping out in the hallways and waiting rooms. There were screaming babies, small kids running in the hallways, and families and patients discussing the most intimate medical information with great theatrics. The circus atmosphere made me crazy, and it seemed like the worst possible environment in which a patient might heal.

We stayed for three days, during which my father remained in his coma. For three days, we heard no other details from my mother, but that he had been found at his work with severe injuries. Blood had been found pouring out of his ears and nose, which we were later told was the result of his skull being crushed. I got no additional information on how his injury had happened, and Astrid and I left after the third day.

My father died two weeks later.

It was not until ten years later that I found out what actually happened to my father. My friend Piet de Vries was a Dutch police officer and he also had a vacation home in Alicante. The Alicante police had called Piet during their investigation into my father's "accident." They had found out that he knew my father, and they had hoped he might have some additional information to contribute. During that time, Piet had been privy to all sorts of information, but he wanted to spare me at that emotional moment. It was his opinion that I first had to work through the bulk of my grief before I could deal with the gruesome reality. Now that so many years had passed, he wanted to tell me the truth.

The truth was that my father had likely been the victim of an attack by ETA. ETA (Euskadi Ta

Askatasuna) is the organization that wants to liberate the Basque region from Spain and France and create an independent Basque nation. I was as confused as I had been before, and I could not see any connection between them and my father.

Piet started to explain, "Well, you know how you occasionally hear about their terrorist attacks, right? ETA is for the Basques what the IRA is for Northern Ireland. And though they call themselves a liberation organization, their practices are those of terrorists."

I was incredulous. "And are you telling me that they murdered my father? But why? My father had nothing to do with the liberation of the Basques, or with their lack of a homeland. Right?"

"You are right, he had no connection to them, not in any political way," answered Piet, "You know your father worked in the warehouse. Well, this place was not just used by the Dutch company he worked for; other boxes would arrive there to be stored as well. Your father was in charge of checking newly arrived boxes and containers. I guess he opened a box he should not have and found weapons. A lot of weapons, enough to outfit a small army."

"You have got to be kidding me!" I could not believe what I was hearing after all those years.

"No, I'm not. Your father told his boss, but apparently his boss already knew all about it. He told your father in no uncertain terms that he was to forget that he had ever seen anything. He should shut up, look the other way, and forget this ever happened. He was told that if he went to the police, there would be terrible consequences."

I imagined the scene and shook my head. "Not a good thing to tell my father"

"What do you mean?"

"My father always spoke his mind, regardless of the consequences, and he had no tolerance for dishonesty. I am sure he went to the police anyway and told them all about it."

"You're right and that decision probably cost him his life. By way of revenge, the owners of those weapons beat him up. They banged his head into the concrete floor long enough so they thought he was dead."

"But he wasn't. When I saw him, he was in a coma."

"You're right, he wasn't quite dead. With his last bit of strength, he crawled outside and then collapsed. Somebody found him and called an ambulance. Unfortunately, it was too late because, as you know, he never regained consciousness."

"But this still makes no sense. Alicante isn't even in the Basque region!"

"Yeah, you're right. But the Basques commit their terrorist acts all over the country." I was grateful to Piet for telling me all this, and though ten years had passed since my father's death, it was still a difficult tale to hear.

The journalists who interviewed me after 9/11 could not have known that terrorists had murdered my father. It's their job to be persistent and to get at the truth, but their grilling was especially hard on me. Sometimes, the only thing they managed to do was to expose their own ignorance. It is quite difficult to figure out if a certain behavior is "suspicious" or not, especially if you don't know what the customs are in the rest of the world. Many of the assumptions journalists made about what was suspicious behavior were incorrect.

First, there was the issue of Atta and Shehhi walking into our facility unannounced. Journalists kept asking me whether that raised any red flags for me. Atta and Shehhi were not only Arabs, but they had walked in under "suspicious" circumstances. Shouldn't their presence have aroused my suspicion?

The answer is no, it wasn't at all suspicious, as Amy Oshier realized on September twelfth. Arabs and other foreigners in Florida who wanted to learn how to fly are actually very common. White, elderly people largely populate Florida, but there are also 220 flight schools that attract people from all over the world. Because of the reliable good weather, it is possible to earn your certification faster here than anyplace else. What takes you two years in the Netherlands, you do here in half a year. On top of that, America had low prices for gasoline, which kept the cost of flying down. Students also save some money because they don't have to pay landing fees like you do in other countries, including Holland. All of these factors meant that flight schools could offer their lessons at a more reasonable cost than they could in other countries. It was actually very common to get students from the Middle East; they often even came in groups of up to ten people.

In fact, through the years, we had so many Muslims at our school that we even set aside a special place for them so that they could pray in comfort and dignity. The morning after the attacks, this option suddenly looked suspicious, but before that time, it was nothing more than our tolerance and hospitality. After all, America is the great melting pot where many people look forward to a peaceful life because people of all colors, religious persuasions, and countries are accepted.

At some point, I received a phone call from a Middle Eastern embassy in Washington, DC, though I can't remember which one it was. The gentleman on the phone said, "Are you Rudi Dekkers, who said on TV that you don't want Muslim students anymore?"

I said, "Yes, sir, I did say that."

He asked, "Would you like you to reconsider that? After all, many Muslims are not terrorists, and what happened was not their fault. These were the actions of an extreme group."

I said, "Sir, I understand your point, but I believe in the 80/20 rule."

He asked me what that was. I explained that if twenty percent of the people create eighty percent of the problems in my company, I don't want to provide services to those people anymore. Unfortunately, they happened to be Muslims. I told him I was sorry, but I would stick to the rule.

However, after my comments about not wanting Muslim students were broadcast to the media, I had at least fifteen death threats over the course of the year. Almost all of the callers had foreign accents, saying they were going to kill me. It is clear to me now that at least one of those people was serious.

The only unusual aspect of the entire situation was that Atta and Shehhi came in person to inquire about our school. How on earth does that translate into full-blown suspicion? One of them looked grumpy, but how should that have alerted me to the fact that I was inviting terrorists into my school? That question was leveled at me again and again during those paranoid days after the attacks.

I was asked if I had become suspicious that Atta had a driver's license. I found out later that long before Atta ever walked onto our facility, he had been flagged as a suspicious character by international security forces and should never have been given a driver's license. Clearly the government had not thought it necessary to monitor him; he was allowed to get a driver's license, take flying lessons, get a student visa, and open a checking account. Nobody ever thought to stop him or warn me.

I told journalists that Atta and Shehhi had paid their first installment for the lessons with a check three days after their registration. One of the reporters focused on their method of payment; why had they not used a credit card? That question, once again, betrayed a lack of knowledge by the journalist of how the rest of the world does business. It is true that if you pay with cash in America, especially when it concerns large purchases, it is considered suspicious. But in our business, and in most of the world, cash payments are very normal, and we had to accept them, even if we did not like them. Most of the foreigners who took classes with us had neither a credit card nor a checking account. They paid for their classes by direct deposit or they cashed traveler checks and paid us in cash.

Atta paid their tuition with checks from the First Union Bank. It was completely legal, and we never had any problem cashing the checks. He always paid one week in advance. The fact that he had an American checking account was actually odd, but still not something that would arouse suspicion. But none of the journalists noticed that Atta and Shehhi having a checking account was actually the thing they should have flagged as "out of the ordinary."

I gave endless tours of my facility. I took the press and their accompanying camera crews around the field. I showed them the Cessna172 with the call number N734EE, the airplane in which Atta flew his first lesson on the seventh of July, 2000 with instructor Thierry Leklou, a native of France. Shehhi took his first forty-five minute flight with Thierry's colleague Mark Mikarts.

I could sense from their reactions and questions how even the most experienced press people flinched at getting so close to the places the terrorists had been. It was frightening for me to see because it clearly showed how polluted Huffman had become. It inspired me to show that I had nothing to hide with even greater conviction.

I was happy to show everyone the classrooms where Atta and Shehhi had studied their theory lessons. Atta had sat in our classroom for 15.8 hours, and Shehhi had needed 21.9 hours to absorb the information he would need to pass his exams. I showed them the flight simulators in which they had to practice flying in bad weather conditions. Ironically, that is the one drawback of taking classes in Florida. There is rarely a bad weather day during which to practice the skills needed to navigate such conditions, so students have to practice under the artificial conditions of a simulator.

The only person at Huffman who later claimed to have had any suspicion was a fellow student, a British woman named Anne Greaves. She called the American Embassy in London on the twelfth of September, 2001, to suggest that the FBI should look in Venice, Florida at Huffman Aviation. Unfortunately, it was much too late, but she claimed that she had always been suspicious of Atta and Shehhi and said she was not surprised at all that they were involved in a terrorist attack. A month later, during an interview with an Australian ABC affiliate, she said that during the six weeks after she began her study in October, 2000, she often had a flight either right before or after Atta and Shehhi. Their paths crossed often, and she had found them distant and unbelievably rude. She found it strange that everybody at Huffman was very enthusiastic about their studies at the school except those two. Atta struck her as a man who had been hypnotized, but in her mind, she had seen him more as a drug runner than a terrorist.

Ms. Greaves said she saw them almost on a daily basis for those six weeks. This was the story she told the reporter:

"They seemed to just come, fly, and then inevitably go into the computer room. They seemed to spend an enormous amount of time, I felt, on the computer, which again irritated me profoundly. The computer was there for students to keep in contact with their families, but also it was there to practice, because we all had to take a theoretical exam in aircraft theory. So the program, which was multiple-choice on the computer, was something that you were supposed to practice yourself. The classroom facilities at Huffman were such that there was a formal classroom, and at the end of that, it was divided off by the computer room by a sort of concertina doors. They were not sound proof, and sometimes I would wait to go into the computer room because Mohamed Atta and Shehhi were using it already. I would just politely wait in the other room, watch a video on aircraft maneuvers or something like that, but you could hear what was going on next door. Now it occurred to me on a few occasions that I thought they're certainly not testing themselves on the program for the theory exam, because it is multiple choice, and you only had to click one key for the right answer. I heard a tremendous amount of activity, finger movements clicking the keys, and it just crossed my mind once or twice, 'my goodness me, they're terribly busy doing whatever communicating with their families or whatever.' They must be doing this extensively and you would hear their hushed voices talking in their own language. And then, there was one occasion, when I thought this was totally out of character. I suddenly heard this outburst of merriment, and I thought, 'my goodness me, you know, so they are human after all,' and I went into the room to see what the merriment was all about and they were both hugging each other, and sort of really slapping each other on the back and laughing. I didn't see the computer screen, so I have no way of knowing what it was that made them so happy and that actually created some emotion. There has been some speculation as to the timing of this, and again I cannot be accurate here with days, but I would say it must have been sometime in October, possibly early in November."

(A suicide bomber attacked the USS Cole while it was harbored in the port of Aden, Yemen on October 12, 2000. The attack was organized by Osama bin Laden. It cost the lives of seventeen sailors.)

I have no idea how much interaction Ms. Greaves had with Muslims outside of Huffman. A lack of understanding of the culture could explain why she was alarmed when most of us were merely annoyed. It is also possible that she was singled out for their special derision because she was a woman. I truly don't know how much weight to give her pronouncements, since she also claimed to have heard from one of her instructors that Atta was of royal blood. When I asked instructors Mike and Thierry if they ever said such a thing, they both denied it.

The story of Atta as prince with Shehhi as his bodyguard was certainly a little overblown. Anyone who needs real protection has a second bodyguard for those times when the first guy is off-duty. She also claimed that Atta was sometimes dressed in a jacket and woolen pants, which might be common in her native Britain, but would be an absurd outfit in the oppressive heat of Florida. Once again, I asked many people about this, but nobody ever saw them wear anything other than T-shirts, jeans, and sneakers.

What Ms. Greaves did observe correctly, along with the rest of us, was that these two guys did not care about their fellow students, and they cut corners wherever they could. The instructors concurred. They learned how to fly, but they were lazy and not too bright—annoying, but not exactly grounds for suspicion.

Vicki, my private secretary, later told me that she had seen both of them drink beer at a nearby bar called the 44th Aero Squadron. The owner of that bar, Ken Schortzmann, later told me that Atta and Shehhi were easy customers. They didn't drink much and didn't bother the waitresses. We know that Muslims are not supposed to drink alcohol at all, so should that have been a warning sign to anybody? Should the bartender have been suspicious? Apparently, Muslims who are about to lose their lives in a suicide attack are allowed to ignore this fundamental law of Islam, but how can you know that this is the reason they are drinking?

Most of the journalists who came to talk to me on September twelfth completely understood my dilemma. There was an awful lot of emotion, but most of them understood that I was merely a businessman, and I had simply done my job. I needed all of my self-defenses during those interviews, the same defenses I had used to survive my abusive childhood.

Despite warnings from my wife, well-meaning friends, and the FBI, the media didn't eat me alive. Most of the people who interviewed me were professional, courteous, and thanked me for taking the time to answer their questions. Each reporter had his or her own style—from Larry King, who was very calm, to Chris Matthews from Hardball, who was extremely nervous and agitated—but almost all treated me with great respect. The Asian television stations even gave little presents to my staff and I, like imprinted ballpoint pens, to thank us for our time, which is apparently their custom.

I had thought the journalists would disappear after about a week, but I was very, very wrong. First of all, nobody was allowed to fly for an entire week, and I was losing tens of thousands of dollars every day because of it. All I was doing all day long was answering questions and staring into the cameras to tell the world that our flight school was innocent. To make things worse for me locally, the Venice Gondolier Sun printed the headline, "Evil in Our Backyard." They also wrote that Huffman has been involved in a number of irregularities and problems. I can only imagine that they were referring to the fact that I was a little late on some of my bills. Nobody bothered to mention that I was employing dozens of people and that my students were good for the local economy. The insane suggestion was that I had something to do with the horrible events of 9/11.

I was terribly upset, but there was nothing I could do. Two months later, I was still talking to journalists and no new students were applying to my school. Ambassador quickly went down the drain. After eight years of hard work, we were finally profitable, but this one event completely wiped us out. On top of that, our chances of getting Florida Air up and running evaporated before my eyes. I worked hard every day, we worked on all sorts of plans, but things were just not going well. Every day brought more journalists and they all wanted to hear the same story. All I could do was to give them what they wanted in the hope that the doom that was hovering over Huffman could be talked away.

The person who owned the World Trade Center towers tried to make some money out of the deal. He decided that each of the planes constituted a separate attack and his insurance company should compensate him twice. After I heard that absurd idea, I called his insurance company; with a little bit of effort, I was able to get somebody on the line. They were a little reluctant, until I told them that I could save them about half of the claim. I explained who I was, that I had known both pilots, and that they were so closely affiliated that there was certainly only one coordinated attempt.

I was never called, but in October 2006 the case was decided both ways. (SR International Business Insurance Company Ltd. versus World Trade Center Properties, LLC, et al.) The federal court upheld an earlier verdict that recognized the two-plane terrorist attacks on the towers at the World Trade Center as a single event for some insurers, but as two events for others. As a result, it held that the attacks were one event under the insurance binder used by major insurers, so WTC developer Larry Silverstein and his Silverstein Properties became entitled to about $4.6 billion. The decision also affirmed a separate jury verdict for nine other insurers that found the event was two claims under a different binder they used while negotiating final coverage terms. The law has a funny way of deciding things.

One of the advantages of talking to so many journalists was that I also got new information every day. I heard the most wide-ranging anecdotes, bizarre details, and conspiracy theories. Peter Jennings, the now deceased reporter, told me that as early as 1995, there had been a plan to hijack planes flying from Hawaii and crash them into San Francisco. Another reporter told me that rescue workers at Ground Zero were walking out with bars of gold hidden in their clothing.

As we all found out more details, to my horror, it turned out that I also knew a third terrorist. The terrorist who kidnapped the flight that ended in a field in Pennsylvania was Ziad Jarrah, a twenty-six-year-old Lebanese man who had taken classes at the Florida Flight Training School. My Dutch competitor and neighbor Arne Kruithof ran that school at the airport in Venice. We saw Ziad regularly because he rented planes from us and often came to pump gas for his planes. Not only was Ziad a very friendly person, but Arne considered him a friend. Ziad accepted Arne's hospitality, went home with him, drank his beer, and ate his barbecue—"friend" indeed.

One of the reporters mentioned that the investigation into Atta and Shehhi revealed that they had met with some Russian people in the Bahamas, one of the places they visited while training at my facility. I immediately called one of my contacts at the FBI and mentioned it to them because I remembered that they had made calls to Russia from Huffman. The FBI then asked for a copy of my phone bill, which I was glad to provide. The list of international calls showed that they had called Russia many times, always to the same number. I never heard anything else about this matter after I gave them my phone bills.

The strangest interview was with Yosri Fouda, an interviewer from Al Jazeera. During the interview, he actually revealed some insider information from Al Qaeda. He proudly told me that he had interviewed Osama bin Laden after 9/11. Apparently it was not that difficult for a reporter to find bin Laden, a feat that, to this day, the entire American military and intelligence community has been unable to accomplish. He happily told me that bin Laden had been very pleased with the attacks. Apparently his engineers made careful calculations that led them to the conclusion that the attack would destroy the top part of the buildings. They were delighted when they saw the buildings completely collapse. It was a success above and beyond their wildest expectations.

This made me revisit the wild theory that there had been explosive charges in the Twin Towers, planted there long before the attacks. The idea was that a mysterious authority, maybe the owner or insurers of the buildings, did not want to take the risk that the buildings would ever topple over. In extreme situations such as 9/11, somebody would then have to make the decision between letting the towers topple over, which would cost the lives of many people in the surrounding area, or to detonate the charges, which would neatly deflate the buildings, "merely" killing the people in and right next to them.

When I questioned how he accessed bin Laden, Mr. Fouda claimed to have been "kidnapped" for a few days by Ramzi Binalshibh and Khalid Sjeik Mohammed, the men who conceived and planned the 9/11 attacks. One must admire his presence of mind to have used his time so diligently with his "kidnappers" to interview them in such depth. It must be difficult to take notes when you are all tied up.

He was interviewing me now for a book he was writing about the events, which he later published. He even sent me a copy of "Masterminds of Terror." Although Fouda pretends that he tried to keep the narrative objective, it still strikes me as obviously pro-Al Qaeda. I was uncomfortable throughout the entire interview with Fouda, and it was unpleasant to have the Al Jazeera crew around me.

A few hours after they left, the FBI called me. They wanted to warn me that someone from Al Jazeera might contact me for an interview. I laughed and told them their warning was a bit too late because he had already been here. I could hear their disappointment, and they asked me if I knew where they had gone. As it happened, I knew exactly where they were staying because they asked my secretary for directions to their hotel. I was happy to pass along the information to the FBI. I hope they all had a pleasant chat.

It is still a mystery to me why Atta and Shehhi bothered getting their commercial pilot's licenses, since much of the information they had to study could not have been of any use to them. Perhaps they had been considering a different plan of attack, one that required other skills. That could be one logical explanation for their interest in crop dusters. I heard from Pedro, a helicopter parts dealer at Miami International, that one of his business partners had sold a crop duster to one of the terrorists. I assumed it was Atta who bought the plane. They might have had a plan to spray one of the big, densely populated cities with some kind of poison. However, crop duster planes are notoriously difficult to handle because of their constantly shifting loads. It is also possible that they were considering loading the crop duster tanks with a flammable substance and then flying them into the World Trade Center, though the plan they settled on was more destructive. In any case, the crop duster had been paid for, but they never came to get it.

Atta and Shehhi went to Miami to learn how to fly the much bigger planes they were thinking of using after I threw them out of my facility in January of 2001. I could assure the journalists that Atta and Shehhi had to learn a whole lot more about flying planes after they left us, because a Boeing or Airbus is a very different plane to fly than a small Cessna. What we taught them would not have provided them enough knowledge to fly into those buildings.

They apparently bought Microsoft Flight Simulator, software that would train them in some of the skills they would eventually need, but didn't learn at Huffman. Just like thousands of flying enthusiasts worldwide, Atta and Shehhi must have practiced with that program for hundreds of hours. Most people spend their time practicing the challenging parts: taking off and landing big planes. Of course, the terrorists had no use for any of that. Professional pilots would handle the takeoff and they never intended to land.

They also bought training time on flight simulators for 747s and 767s in Dakota, Georgia, and with SimCenter in the Opa-Locka airport, about ten miles north of Miami, Florida, where they paid $1,500 for six hours in a Boeing 727 flight simulator. The inside of a flight simulator is a completely accurate copy of the inside of a real cockpit. The simulator is mounted on hydraulic pumps and gives a student an accurate feeling for how the real plane will handle. It is no replacement for the actual experience, but it does provide valuable experience. Henry George, the owner of that machine, told the Miami Herald, "In retrospect, it was odd that all they wanted was practice turns..." It might have been odd, but nobody thought it strange enough to report to authorities.

Things have changed since 9/11. Previously, anyone with a pilot's license and the money to pay the bill could use the simulators. The government has passed legislation since then that prohibits flight schools from training inexperienced pilots on heavy aircraft simulators. Now, only experienced pilots who want additional training can use the simulators, and only after a thorough background check.

In addition to gaining mastery over the steering mechanism, Atta and Shehhi had to know the location of specific instrumentation. They learned the location of the autopilot, as well as how to disengage it from the computer flight simulator. The simulator program also taught them how to locate and turn off the transponder, a piece of equipment that sends a code to the air traffic controllers on the ground so they know which blip corresponds to which plane on their screen. Turning this off would make their plane harder to follow from the ground as the plane would then show up as a generic blip.

Then there was the issue of navigation. I can only imagine that they brought their own hand-held GPS devices when they hijacked the planes. That is how they must have known where to steer the plane to reach the World Trade Center. From what I have heard, the one mistake Atta made was concerning one of the instruments on the planes. At one point, he was looking to maintain order on his plane and was trying to use the intercom system to tell the passengers that everybody should stay calm and that he was going to land the plane. Instead, he was talking to the air traffic tower. Supposedly, there is a recording of that announcement.

I also heard about an interesting experiment conducted in Amsterdam, in which ten professional pilots who worked for major airlines, all of whom had thousands of hours of flying experience to their names, were invited for a test. They were invited to spend some time in a flight simulator, which was a very familiar experience for all these men. Their task was simple: with the same plane, location, weather conditions, and airspeed, they were told to hit the towers. Nine out of the ten participants were not able to crash the airplane into the tower. It's actually much more difficult than you might think. The planes are very large, which makes course corrections very slow. They also are flying at great speeds, which give the pilots a very small margin of error. As a pilot, I believe there was also one other factor at play. All pilot training is focused on safety for yourself, for your plane, and for other objects. It is unnatural for a professional pilot to throw out all that training and do the complete opposite.

Along with the rest of the world, I found out the terrorists' missions came close to failing several times. After Ziad Jarrah flew back from an Al Qaeda training camp in Afghanistan, he was stopped in Dubai on orders of the CIA. He was questioned and released. After one of his visits to Europe, Atta was stopped in Miami with an expired visa, but he was still admitted. On April 26, 2001, the police stopped him for erratic driving. He was given a warning and told to appear in court. He did not show up in court, and even though he was registered in the state of Florida and could easily have been found, no further action was taken. On June fifth, he was stopped again, this time for speeding. The police officer gave him a ticket, but somehow did not find Atta's previous violation when he checked the registration information. If he had found the previous violation, he would have arrested Atta. Who knows how many other times they slipped through the net.

Through all of the interviews, I had only a few negative experiences with the media. Ironically, one was with a Dutch reporter whose interview style was very aggressive. He kept trying to force me to say things I did not mean, and in the end, he took my words completely out of context. I told him that if the planes had not hit the buildings, they might have done even more damage by going down in the streets of Manhattan, taking out a block or two of buildings and the people in them. He twisted that around to make it sound as if I had said I was happy the planes hit the buildings. I had heard this complaint about Dutch journalists before, and it was very disappointing to see my own country have so little commitment to the truth. It was particularly offensive to me, as a Dutch person, to be vilified in a well-known Dutch magazine.

The other bad apple was a person who maintains a website through which he sells sensationalist books. Accusations are strange things, so let me try to explain. This is the question at hand: how can you prove you did *not* do something? If I accused you of having had intimate relations with a hippopotamus, how would you prove you did not? I could say I saw you in a zoo;

I'm sure you visited a zoo at some point in your life, so that would be true. I could mention that you are known to watch animal shows on TV. I can say I find it an odd coincidence that you are the only person on your block who can spell hippopotamus, and that all this makes it obvious that you are guilty. Go ahead, prove me wrong! Make no mistake about it, I can call myself an "investigative journalist" and publish that crazy story about you on the Internet. When a story like that hits the web, it acquires an air of legitimacy. Because it is a funny story, it will show up on web sites that specialize in outrageous stuff. People click on it and read it, and the more people read it, the more popular it becomes. The most popular articles are the ones on the first page on search engines like Google. When someone does a search for your name, the story about you and the fat zoo animal comes up for the first five pages. At some point, even a Google search for "hippopotamus" starts to yield, and the story pops up right after the National Geographic Special, your name and this idiotic story. Every schoolchild doing a report now knows about you and your filthy habit. Next time you apply for a job, try to get a date, or a loan, this is the story everybody reads about you. You tell me how that affects your life!

Here is a highlight from the bizarre stories about me. There is a claim that a cab driver says that I went with Atta to a strip bar. What can I say to such a weird lie? I was never in a cab with Atta, I never went to a strip joint with Atta, and I never went out to drink with Atta. Even casual acquaintances know that I do not drink because of my extremely negative childhood association with drinking.

Because of all the media attention surrounding my terrorist students, my web site got around 500,000 hits a day for the first couple of months, and we received hundreds of thousands of e-mails. We couldn't even open them. The flood jammed the e-mail, and we had to destroy most of them because we were not set up to handle that kind of volume. I did read a few emails before we had to delete all of them; I found some hate mail, but also many supportive messages. I have to hand it to my office manager Susan Desantis. She handled herself like the professional she is and did an amazing job throughout that stressful time. During the first couple of weeks, she had her hands full handling the phone, including the hate calls accusing us of being responsible for the attacks. Once the media published my side of the story, some people realized that we had no way of knowing that they had been terrorists and that we weren't responsible. A few even called back to apologize.

I would like to thank all the people who supported me at that time. I'm sorry I could not respond to each of you individually, but I thank you for your kindness. It meant a lot to me then and now. And I hope those who thought I did something wrong will read this book and understand the situation and realize that there was no way I could have known.

THE TERRORISTS GET THEIR VISAS

On March 11, 2002, two envelopes landed on my desk from the INS. Over the years, I have received a lot of material from the INS, both for myself and for all the international students in our school, so it came as no surprise. I opened the envelopes without a great deal of expectation, but when I looked at the pieces of paper, I could hardly believe what I held in my hands. Almost six months after Atta and Shehhi flew their planes into the World Trade Center, the INS saw fit to hand them their student visas! I happened to have a CNN reporter there, so I told them what I had just received. They did not show a great deal of enthusiasm for the material, but they made a note of it. Amy Oshier from the local NBC affiliate called a little while later, but when I told her about the visas, she came over immediately to see the documents. She made sure the world heard about it.

A couple of hours later, Susan called me from the front desk and said there was a man asking for me. I said I was somewhat busy and asked if he could come back.

"No, I don't think so," she said. "It is someone from the INS."

By now I was used to the FBI men and women who came dressed in business attire, but this man was dressed very casually, wearing a short-sleeve Hawaiian shirt. He said he wanted me to hand over the visas from Atta and Shehhi.

I said, "Are you serious? I have never seen your agency move this quickly on any matter!" Evidently, the president had been on TV saying he was "hot" about the situation. It still seemed like an odd request, so I asked, "What if I don't want to give them to you?"

He answered, "Well, you can either give them to me now, or I have a subpoena here for them, which is not yet signed, but which I can get signed fairly quickly."

I decided not to make any trouble and handed him the documents. He told me I wasn't allowed to make copies of the visas. I laughed because I couldn't imagine why I would need to make copies of their visas, but by the end of the day, I had an offer from the National Enquirer for $500,000 for them. I think about that offer sometimes, because that money would have saved Huffman Aviation.

A few days later, I received a phone call from Art Arthur of the House of Representatives in Washington, DC. He said, "Mr. Dekkers, we would like you to testify in Congress."

I agreed, and he told me the subcommittee would hold an oversight hearing at four p.m. on Tuesday, March 19, 2002, at the Rayburn House office building. The hearing was on "The INS March 2002 Notification of Approval of Change of Status for Pilot Training for Terrorist Hijackers Mohammed Atta and Marwan al-Shehhi." In the follow-up letter, they asked me to come to Washington to testify before Congress, and for a written statement. They also told me they needed a hundred copies of my statement. I called them back and told them I'd be happy to give them a written statement, but was sure they could figure out how to get a hundred copies made.

I have reproduced a copy of that letter in this book to show that I was invited to testify. I was not subpoenaed, nor were any documents subpoenaed. Most journalists get that detail wrong and I want to set the record straight.

An FBI agent called me up shortly after that and said, "Rudi, do you know we forgot to do an official interview with you? We talked so many times, but we don't have an official written testimony from you in our files. Can we still do that?" They had all the information, of course, but they had never bothered to get my official statement. It is one of the many ways I know that I was never under any suspicion by the FBI.

Then the Department of Justice in Washington, DC, called and said they wanted my testimony, and I should not talk to any other agency before I talked to them. I told them I was already scheduled to go to Washington to testify before Congress. The caller was very insistent and said he needed my statement first. I was told an agent would call to set it up. A little while later, Agent Marino called me up from Miami.

He was very pleasant and asked, "Mr. Dekkers, when can we see you?"

I said, "I have some time tomorrow; I can see you at two."

That was good for him, too, and so he asked if I

needed directions on how to get to the office in Miami. I told him that I certainly knew how to get to Miami, but I didn't have time to go there. The way I had understood it was that they wanted to see me, and they should feel welcome to come see me the next day.

He started to get a bit nasty, saying, "We are interviewing you, Mr. Dekkers. You are not interviewing us!"

I said that I was very sorry, but this was not the message I had from Washington. He didn't like that at all. I was sorry about that, too, but said he should call Washington to get the full picture and call back a couple of hours later.

In the meantime, I got to thinking, "Oh, my Lord, this is going to be an interview with the Department of Justice; I should probably be represented by an attorney." I called my immigration attorney in Naples and told him what was happening. I asked him if it would be better if we did the interview in his office. He agreed, and we set up a date. In the end, they were very pleasant. I told them my whole story and they were satisfied.

On March 19, 2002, I flew to Washington, DC in my own plane. My son-in-law Shawn and his friend Rene flew me to Washington. I remember that it was a terrible flight with lousy weather conditions, and I have already told you how nervous that makes me. We could not land in Washington, DC because of flight restrictions, so we landed at Montgomery County Airpark near Gaithersburg, MD. Before I went to Congress, I did a live national interview, and then I walked over to the House of Representatives.

Among the other people testifying that day were Mr. James W. Ziglar, Commissioner of the Immigration and Naturalization Service; Mr. Tom Blodgett, managing director of Business Process Solutions for Affiliated Computer Services, Incorporated, the company the INS contracts with to process visas; and Mr. Michael Cutler, a special agent from the New York District Office of the Immigration and Naturalization Service. The meeting started at four in the afternoon with a blistering criticism by The Honorable Elton Gallegly, a Representative in Congress from the State of California, who blasted the INS for incompetence and even outright dishonesty.

In another opening statement, I was surprised to hear Anthony D. Weiner, New York, state that one of the things he thought was wrong regarding the whole situation was that, "you can actually take lessons in flying planes without having to learn how to land them." That was one of the many common but utterly incorrect rumors that were spread at the time. It was a surprise to me that even a highly informed man like Mr. Weiner did not know that the FAA would not allow anybody to fly solo, let alone get their license, if they could not land the plane.

Mr. Ziglar had only been at his job in the INS for nine months. He defended his agency's record as best he could, considering the mess he had just inherited. He was often interrupted, and he must have felt a great deal of frustration at the way the hearing went.

I will reprint some of the testimony from Mr. Blodgett, who was the managing director of ACS, the company that actually sent me the visas. It explains, in technical terms, how things were handled:

> In August 2000, Huffman Aviation filed I-20 applications with INS to change Atta's and Shehhi's visas from tourist to student status. INS approved the requested changes in July and August 2001. On September 24, 2001, ACS received the completed I-20 forms for microfilm, data entry, and storage for the mandatory 180-day period. ACS processed the I-20 forms and returned the microfilm and electronic data back to INS and stored the forms as required by contract. The BPA changing the 180-day storage period to a 30-day storage period went into effect December 18, 2001 for I-20 forms processed on and after that date. The I-20 forms then in 180-day storage continued in that status until February 27, 2002 when INS requested that ACS begin mailing all of the I-20 forms then held in 180-day storage status to the form originators. On March 5, 2002, ACS did an automated bulk mailing of approximately 4,000 I-20 forms. The Huffman Aviation forms for Atta and Shehhi were part of the 180-day storage and were mailed to Huffman Aviation as part of the March 5, 2002, mailing.

The real question was, of course, why these forms were in 180-day storage in the first place and not processed immediately, the way they are now. But that is a question for the bureaucrats to answer. The most important thing was that the visas had been approved for six months before they were sent to me.

I will reprint my entire testimony so that you can see

what I told them. As you can see, it includes a prepared statement, which is customary in these hearings. (Some mistakes were fixed to make these statements easier to understand.)

Good afternoon, Mr. Chairman and Members. Thank you for asking me here. I feel like I don't belong on this table because I just own a small flight school. But anyway, I will give you my testimony. I will concern my five minutes or a couple minutes to talk to you about the INS matter.

When Atta and Shehhi came to my facility on July 1, they inquired information about how much they have to pay, et cetera, about flying. That is a different situation than normal. Normally, foreign students are calling, inquiring over the Internet from their home countries overseas. When they inquire for that information, we send them that. After a while, they get back to us and state they want to fly with us. We send them an I-20 form. We fill out the form according to the course they're going to follow. We send that form to the students. They go to their United States Consulate in their country. The United States Consulate checks out the information. If there's enough funds, if the person is really the person, then the consulate stamps it and the student takes it with him to the border. The border will see the I-20 form and the student can continue.

That's a different situation. Atta and Shehhi came through my front door. When I have foreigners coming in—and I'm a foreigner myself; I'm a guest in this country—I ensure that the rules are watched a bit more than if I were an American. Why? Because I want to do it by the book.

As a flight school, we know that when a student walks in and they want to fly a professional flight course, and they're continuing studying, so they're not part-time, they need to have a change of status. By the way, a change of status needs to be filled out by the student, by the individual, not by the school. The school has the obligation to send in an I-20 form in case it's an M1 student visa. We determined that, since Atta had a B-1/B-2 visa and Shehhi had a tourist visa, we wanted to go for the M1 because they were not part time, they were full time. There are a lot of rules in FAA-INS; you could train these people even without an M1. My only reason for being happy about receiving these forms was that I could show the world we asked for an M1 visa.

So I want to specifically tell you that this case is different than normal because they came in the front door. We sent two I-20 forms to Texas INS, and we had the approval receipts from ACS. So it's a little bit of a different scenario than a normal scenario.

This is what I have to say. Thank you, Mr. Chairman.

PREPARED STATEMENT OF RUDI DEKKERS

On July 1, 2000, Mohamed Atta and Marwan al-Shehhi arrived at Huffman Aviation in Venice, Florida, to inquire about taking flying lessons. After a description was given about our flying school, they said they would let us know what they would decide about the flying lessons.

On July 3, 2000, Atta and Shehhi came back to Huffman Aviation to sign up for lessons. Atta already held a Private Pilot License but wanted to advance and get his Commercial License, and Shehhi was there to obtain both a Private and Commercial License. They had stated they were unhappy with a flying school they attended up north.

We told them the cost for the licenses they wanted was about $18,000 per person, with a $1,000 down payment and $1,000 weekly thereafter, paid by Atta with a check drawn from a First Union account.

They inquired about a place to stay. It is normal procedure for a flying school to offer proper accommodations for students learning to fly. However, at the time, Huffman Aviation had no such accommodations, because they came through the front door without advance notice for Huffman Aviation to take care of a room. Rudi Dekkers, owner of Huffman Aviation, knew that Charles Voss, CFO of Huffman Aviation, rented out rooms in his home. Atta and Shehhi rented a room from Voss, but after one week were asked to leave due to excessive rudeness from Atta to Mrs. Voss. After their eviction, there was no mention of where they were staying.

Atta and Shehhi started their flying lessons on July 6, 2000, in a Cessna 172, N734EE, with flight instructor, Thierry Leklou. In August, Leklou went to the chief flight instructor, Dan Purcell, to complain that Atta and Shehhi had behavioral problems and were not following instructions. They also had bad attitudes. Purcell asked Dekkers if it would be okay to expel them from the program. Dekkers said that if necessary, *it would be acceptable to expel them from the program. Purcell had a meeting with both Atta and Shehhi to let them know there had been complaints about their behavior and that if they would not conform, they would have to leave the program. Their behavior changed, and they were able to continue their lessons without any further problems throughout the course. On August 29, 2000, Nicky Antini, Student Coordinator of Huffman Aviation, sent in I-20Ms to the INS, along with a copy of their passports.*

Dekkers, on many occasions, tried to communicate with Atta, but Atta was very unfriendly with everyone. Dekkers knew that Atta had lived in Hamburg, Germany, and one day spoke to him in German as a way of friendly communication. Atta was stunned and quickly walked away. Shehhi, on the other hand, was very friendly and willing to communicate with everyone. He always seemed to walk behind Atta; we had the impression that Atta and Shehhi were family.

In December 2000, Atta and Shehhi took their last flight tests. Atta had approximately 270 hours of total flight time and received his Instrument, Single/Multi-Commercial Certification. Shehhi was granted the same certification along with a Private Pilot License. Dave Whitman, the local FAA designated examiner, gave them their exams, which they passed with average grades, and they were given temporary FAA licenses for 120 days.

On December 24, 2000, Atta and Shehhi rented a Warrior (N555HA) from Huffman Aviation for a flight. They landed in Miami; the engine stalled (shut off) on the taxiway, where they abandoned it. They called Huffman Aviation for taxi fare back to Venice but were denied by Huffman Aviation. One to two days later, Huffman received a phone call from the Miami FAA regarding the Warrior that had been unattended for a half-hour on the runway. Dekkers got in contact with Bob Martin, the Operations Manager of Huffman Aviation, who then contacted the FAA. Martin had several phone conversations with the FAA, and upon their request sent all maintenance records on the Warrior to the FAA. Nothing else was reported from the FAA to Huffman regarding the Warrior.

Atta and Shehhi returned to Huffman Aviation to make final payments on their outstanding bills. Atta paid a total of $18,703.50 and Shehhi paid a total of $20,917.63. Because they were not taking any more flying lessons, they were asked to leave the facility due to their bad attitudes and not being liked by staff and clients alike. Huffman never heard about or from them again until September 11, 2001.

On September 12, 2001, at 3:00 a.m, the FBI Chief Investigator Kelly J. Thomas called Huffman's general manager, Dale Krauss, to help them with files on Atta and Shehhi. Krauss was no longer working for Huffman Aviation so Krauss gave the FBI Susan Desantis' phone number who was Dekkers' assistant. Desantis arrived at Huffman at 4:00 a.m. to give the FBI the files on Atta and Shehhi. Desantis asked if she should call Dekkers, the FBI told her this was not necessary. At 7:00 a.m., while the FBI was still looking over the files and computers, Desantis called Dekkers, who was shocked and annoyed he had not been contacted earlier. The FBI waited for Dekkers upon Dekkers' request. Dekkers immediately left for Huffman from Bonita Springs, Florida. Dekkers let the FBI know there were more Muslim student files. Therefore, the FBI ended up taking over 100 files and two computers. Dekkers informed the FBI he also owned a flight school in Naples, Florida, named Ambassador Airways. This furthered no reaction.

Several days after September 11, 2001, the Naples FBI contacted Dekkers and asked for files from students. The FBI asked if Dekkers could recognize the other terrorists. Dekkers did not recognize any other terrorist. The FBI took several files and returned them about three months later.

On Friday, March 8, 2002, a meeting had been set up with CNN Miami to do an interview regarding the six-month anniversary of September 11, 2001, for Monday, March 11, 2002. Dekkers opened the mail that Monday morning to discover the original I-20Ms (student visa applications) for Atta and Shehhi. It had been over a year since Atta and Shehhi left Huffman Aviation and six months since their deaths. Dekkers was relieved to see the paperwork but not surprised. It usually took a long time for visas to be returned from the INS. Dekkers was relieved because now he could prove that his company had carried out the proper procedures regarding Atta and Shehhi's I-20Ms. Huffman had previously been castigated for not following proper procedures. This new information was brought to the attention of CNN.

On Thursday, March 14, 2002, President Bush gave a press conference and answered a question regarding the I-20Ms that had arrived at Huffman Aviation. He replied there would be a full investigation. At 4:30 p.m. that day, an INS officer from Tampa arrived at Huffman requesting that all original documents be returned. Dekkers was more than willing to cooperate with the government but was reluctant to surrender the documents until a subpoena was produced by the INS officer from his briefcase. Dekkers immediately surrendered the documents.

On the way back home to Bonita Springs, Florida on Thursday, March 14, 2002, Dekkers received a phone call from the office of the Assistant General Attorney, Mr. Marino. Marino wanted to discuss the entire incident and asked if Dekkers would bring along the original I-20Ms on Friday, March 15, 2002. Marino was surprised to discover that Dekkers was no longer in possession of the original documents, which were taken by the INS. A meeting has been set up for Dekkers and Marino to meet on Monday, March 18, 2002, at 12:00 p.m. in Naples, Florida.

What was so frustrating to me about the Congressional hearing was that it was all about politics and finding somebody or something to blame. Nobody was there to brainstorm a solution. I was hoping I could offer some ideas based on my experience in the aviation industry that would make it safer, but apparently this hearing was not designed for that. At the end, I said again that I would like an opportunity to speak, and though they said it was unusual to speak when not asked, the chairperson gave me a few moments. As you can see, I only got the opportunity to make a brief comment.

Mr. DEKKERS: There's—can I say something, Mr. Chairman? Can I say——

Mr. GEKAS: Yes, quickly.

Mr. DEKKERS: I heard Mr. Ziglar saying about two hours ago that he would stop letting students come into the country to fly professional flight courses on a tourist visa. We applaud that in the industry. We think that our pilot industry—we are 70 to 80 percent down. A lot of us are going bankrupt right now. I think that we would like to work together with the government. We are also helping with protection. If we got somebody at our doorstep, we followed up the M–1. But eighty percent of the flight schools are non-approved flight schools. They have never heard about an M–1. So we, as an industry, would like to work with the government and to see how we can help each other.

Mr. GEKAS: The time of the Chair has expired.

I felt that, because my testimony had revealed some incompetency at the INS and the Department of Homeland Security, from that day on, there was a black mark on my name and both agencies would do whatever they could to make things difficult for me. But it was great to hear Mr. Ziglar say, "I want to make it clear that Mr. Dekkers did nothing wrong in his business," a statement he repeated one more time. I am deeply grateful to him for emphasizing that to the committee.

The headlines in the newspapers the next day were wonderful. They loudly proclaimed, "Dekkers did it by the book," and the articles about the hearing made it clear that not only was I not to blame, I had been following the law. That headline and those articles helped me a lot and business started to pick up a little after that. The change in atmosphere after the media reports of my testimony to Congress showed me how powerful of an influence the media is on people's perceptions.

When the 9/11 report came out, I was not surprised to find my name mentioned. However, I was quite surprised that they did not get their facts right. In section 7.2, they published:

In mid-September, Atta and Shehhi applied to change their immigration status from tourist to student, stating their intention to study at Huffman until September 1, 2001. In late September, they decided to enroll at Jones Aviation in Sarasota, Florida, about twenty miles north of Venice. According to the instructors at Jones, the two were aggressive, rude, and sometimes even fought with him to take over the controls during their training flights. In early October, they took the Stage 1 exam for instrument rating at Jones Aviation and failed. Very upset, they said they were in a hurry because jobs awaited them at home. Atta and Shehhi returned to Huffman.

If you've read this far, you know this is simply not accurate. The error does not matter to me, but it does make me shudder to think how many other "facts" in the official report are just as misleading.

Immigration and Naturalization Service — Status For Vocational Students — OMB No. 1115-0051

This page must be completed and signed in the U.S. by a designated school official.

Family name (surname): Alshehhi
First (given) name (do not enter middle name): Marwan
Country of birth: UAE
Date of birth (mo./day/year): 05/09/78
Country of citizenship: UAE
Admission number (complete if known):
School (school district) name: Huffman Aviation International
School official to be notified of student's arrival in U.S. (Name and Title): Nicole Antini, Student Coordinator
School address (include zip code): 400 East Airport Avenue Venice, FL 34285
School code (include 3-digit suffix, if any) and approval date: MIA _____ 214F 1096.00 Approved on 06/22/90

For Immigration Only Use
APPROVED
AUG 09 2001
SSC 5..7
Visa issuing post: M-1 to 10-1-20 (E)
Date visa issued:
Reinstated, extension granted to: SRC-01-276-50854

3. This certificate is issued to the student named above for: *(check and fill out as appropriate)*
   a. ☐ Initial attendance at this school.
   b. ☒ Continued attendance at this school.
   c. ☐ School transfer. Transferred from _____
   d. ☐ Use by dependents for entering the United States.
   e. ☐ Other _____

4. Level of education the student is pursuing or will pursue in the United States: *(Check only one)*
   a. ☐ High school   b. ☒ Other vocational school

5. The student named above has been accepted for a full course of study at this school, majoring in Pro. Pilot Prg.
   The student is expected to report to the school not later than (date) 09/01/00 and complete studies not later than (date) 09/01/01 the normal length of study is 12 Months

6. ☒ English proficiency is required:
   ☒ The student has the required English proficiency.
   ☐ The student is not yet proficient. English instructions will be given at the school.
   ☐ English proficiency is not required because _____

7. This school estimates the student's average costs for an academic term of 12 MO. (up to 12) months to be:
   a. Tuition and fees $ 18,000.00
   b. Living expenses $ 9,300.00
   c. Expenses of dependents $ _____
   d. Other (specify): $ _____
                   Total $ 27,300.00

8. This school has information showing the following as the student's means of support, estimated for an academic term of months (Use the same number of months given in item 7).
   a. Students personal funds $ 27,300.00
   b. Funds from this school (specify type): $ _____
   c. Funds from another source (specify type and source): $ _____
                   Total $ 27,300.00

9. Remarks: _____

School Certification: I certify under penalty of perjury that all information provided above in items 1 through 8 was completed before I signed this form and is true and correct; I executed this form in the United States after review and evaluation in the United States by me or other officials of the school of the student's application, transcripts or other records of grades taken and proof of financial responsibility which were received at the school prior to the execution of this form; the school has determined that the above named student's qualifications meet all standards for admission to the school; the student will be required to pursue a full course of study as defined by 8 CFR 214.2(f)(6); I am a designated official of the above named school and I am authorized to issue this form.

Signature of designated school official: *Nicole Antini*
Name of designated school official & title (print or type): Nicole Antini, Student Co.
Date and place issued (city and state): 08/29/00 Venice, FL

Student Certification: I have read and agreed to comply with the terms and conditions of my admission and those of any extension of stay as specified on page 2. I certify that all information provided on this form refers to me and is true and correct to the best of my knowledge. I certify that I seek to enter or remain in the United States temporarily, and solely for the purpose of pursuing a full course of study at the school named on item 2 of this form. I also authorize the named school to release any information from my records which is needed by the INS pursuant to 8 CFR 214.3(g).

Signature of student: _____   Name of student (print or type): Marwan Alshehhi   Date: _____
Signature of parent or guardian (if student is under 18): _____   Name of parent or guardian (print or type): _____   Date: _____
Address of parent or guardian: _____ (street) _____ (city) _____ (state or province) _____ (county)

Form I-20M-N/I-20ID Copy (Rev. 5-2-90)N

For official use only
Microfilm Index Number

U.S. Department of Justice
Immigration and Naturalization Service

Certificate of Eligibility for Nonimmigrant (M-1) Student Status–For Vocational Students

OMB No. 1115-0051

This page must be completed and signed in the U.S. by a designated school official.

Family name (surname): Atta
First (given) name (do not enter middle name): Mohamed
Country of birth: Egypt
Date of birth (mo./day/year): 09/01/68
Country of citizenship: Egypt
Admission number (complete if known):
School (school district) name: Huffman Aviation International
School official to be notified of student's arrival in U.S. (Name and Title): Nicole Antini, Student Coordinator
School address (include zip code): 400 East Airport Avenue Venice, FL 34285
School code (include 3-digit suffix, if any) and approval date: MIA 214F 1096.000 Approved on 06/22/90

For Immigration Only Use
APPROVED
JUL 17 2001
SSC
Manuel Alvarez

Visa issuing post: M-1 to
Date visa issued: 10-01-2003 G
Reinstated, extension granted to:
SRC-00-276-50863

3. This certificate is issued to the student named above for: (check and fill out as appropriate)
   a. ☐ Initial attendance at this school.
   b. ☒ Continued attendance at this school.
   c. ☐ School transfer. Transferred from _____
   d. ☐ Use by dependents for entering the United States.
   e. ☐ Other _____

4. Level of education the student is pursuing or will pursue in the United States: (Check only one)
   a. ☐ High school   b. ☒ Other vocational school

5. The student named above has been accepted for a full course of study at this school, majoring in Pro. Pilot Prg.
   The student is expected to report to the school not later than (date) 09/01/00 and complete studies not later than (date) 09/01/01 the normal length of study is _____

6. ☒ English proficiency is required:
   ☒ The student has the required English proficiency.
   ☐ The student is not yet proficient, English instructions will be given at the school.
   ☐ English proficiency is not required because _____

7. This school estimates the student's average costs for an academic term of 12 mo. (up to 12) months to be:
   a. Tuition and fees $ 18,000.00
   b. Living expenses $ 9,300.00
   c. Expenses of dependents $
   d. Other (specify): $
                       Total $ 27,300.00

8. This school has information showing the following as the student's means of support, estimated for an academic term of months (Use the same number of months given in item 7).
   a. Student's personal funds $ 27,300.00
   b. Funds from this school (specify type): $
   c. Funds from another source (specify type and source): $
                                    Total $ 27,300.00

9. Remarks: _____

School Certification: I certify under penalty of perjury that all information provided above in items 1 through 8 was completed before I signed this form and is true and correct; I executed this form in the United States after review and evaluation in the United States by me or other officials of the school of the student's application, transcripts or other records of courses taken and proof of financial responsibility which were received at the school prior to the execution of this form; the school has determined that the above named student's qualifications meet all standards for admission to the school; the student will be required to pursue a full course of study as defined by 8 CFR 214.2(f)(6); I am a designated official of the above named school and I am authorized to issue this form.

Signature of designated school official: Nicole Antini
Name of designated school official & title (print or type): Nicole Antini, Student Coord.
Date and place issued (city and state): 08/29/00 Venice, FL

Student Certification: I have read and agreed to comply with the terms and conditions of my admission and those of any extension of stay as specified on page 2. I certify that all information provided on this form refers to me and is true and correct to the best of my knowledge. I certify that I seek to enter or remain in the United States temporarily, and solely for the purpose of pursuing a full course of study at the school named on item 2 of this form. I also authorize the named school to release any information from my records which is needed by the INS pursuant to 8 CFR 214.3(g).

Signature of student: _____
Name of student (print or type): Mohamed Atta
Date: _____

Signature of parent or guardian (if student is under 18): _____
Name of parent or guardian (print or type): _____
Date: _____

Address of parent or guardian: _____ (street) _____ (city) _____ (state or province) _____ (county)

Form I-20M-N/I-20ID Copy (Rev. 6-3-90)N

For official use only
Microfilm Index Number

FALLOUT

It's been a neverending surprise to me how people have reacted to me after 9/11. There were people who went out of their way to support and help me. And there were also people and agencies who could have helped and had no reason not to help, but who made things as miserable for me as possible. There is nothing quite like a crisis to find out who your true friends are.

At the beginning of September 2001, I was doing really well. I had forty-five planes at my flight school in Naples and I was finally in the black. But, within a month after 9/11, I had to close down Ambassador Airways in Naples. I had a huge payroll there; my income went from making $100,000 gross income per month to $10,000, but of course my expenses did not go down. This huge drop was because the SFT flight school in England, which sent me many international students, went bankrupt. The reason was simple and could not have been anything any of us could have foreseen. They had a policy that required students to pay their entire tuition in advance. Immediately after 9/11, all those parents asked for their money back because they did not want their sons and daughters to go to flight school in the United States. But the school had already spent that money to buy new planes and upgrade their equipment. In England, the law is that a company owner had three choices: pay his bills immediately, which now included all these refunds, declare bankruptcy, or be personally responsible for the bills. The guy called me and said, "Rudi, I have to declare bankruptcy; I owe more than 200,000 pounds to all these people." He owed me money, too, but I never got a cent.

It took me ten years to put the deal together with SFT and in just a few days, it was gone. I had no choice and told everybody, "This is the end; we're closing up shop." The company that I built from 1993 to 2001—years of blood, sweat, and tears—was gone. That was difficult, really difficult. The banks took back all the planes, and because I had a lot of equity built up the banks were paid off. But I personally lost one million dollars in that company.

Shortly after 9/11, the DOT contacted the Florida Air company lawyer and told him, "If Rudi Dekkers does not resign as CEO and president of Florida Air, the company will never get its permits to fly." I was devastated. In the board meeting, I said I would resign and stay as a shareholder only. I had 24.9% of the shares, but the DOT wanted me out and told me I could not be a shareholder, either. The DOT even said that I could not be in the building where the airline was located, even though I owned that building. When my lawyer asked why they were so adamant that I have no connection with the airline, they said it was very simple: because I was involved in the 9/11 attack. No matter how ridiculous this is, the DOT can do what it wants. If you don't comply with their demands, no matter how absurd, they will simply not give you a permit.

I gave my shares to my partner, Wally Hilliard, who had been a friend for a long time and was someone I thought I could trust. After everything calmed down and the airline was flying, he would give me my shares back, which would have a value of about $1.5 million. However, the new president for Florida Air was completely incompetent, and with his "help," the airline never made it any further. Two years later, it was sold to a company in Nevada and most of the investors lost their money. I lost everything I had invested, too: five years of hard work and a lot of money. I was left with just Huffman Aviation in Venice, and I was doing what I could to keep that alive.

After 9/11, I had TV stations there every day. They all asked me, "So how are things going?" I would tell them the truth, which was that things were not going well. The one income-producing part of Huffman Aviation I still had was selling aviation fuel, but I was not selling enough fuel to keep the business afloat. I sat down to think. It was true that business was bad, but I knew that if you say something often enough and with enough emotion, you create your own reality. I simply decided to start saying something different.

The next time somebody asked me how things were going, I said, "You know, it's an interesting thing: the day after I testified in Congress, the headlines read, 'Rudi did it by the book.' Things are getting better and jets are showing up to buy fuel."

Wouldn't you know, at exactly that moment, a jet showed up for fuel. It was the first time that had happened. A week later, somebody else asked me how things were going and I said, "The jets are showing up, and the captains are saying, 'Hey, if we can support Rudi Dekkers from Huffman Aviation, we will do that.'"

I will never know what came first, the chicken or the egg, but I suddenly started to sell fuel. Now I had a different problem. Cash flow was a big issue—I didn't have enough cash to buy a full truckload of fuel. I called Jones Aviation, about twelve miles away at Sarasota airport. Since we were longtime friends, I felt free to make a rather odd request and asked him, "May I buy fuel from you for a decent price?" He was a good man and willing to help me out. He said, "All I need is a dime per gallon over what I pay." It was a very kind and generous offer. I sent over my fuel truck, and I only had to pay for 1,200 gallons at a time, which was manageable.

We drove our truck to Sarasota about three or four times before somebody called the Venice Airport Authority to complain. We hadn't realized that it was illegal to drive the truck on the regular roads; it had no regular license plates since it normally only drove around the airport. The Airport Authority called us and said, "You cannot do that; it's illegal. If we catch you, we will have to report you to the police." But I really needed that fuel and I still didn't have the cash to buy a full delivery myself. I thought of a new idea. I rented a trailer and carried the fuel truck on the top of the trailer; it looked pretty ridiculous. But we had to survive, so we were creative. The guys at Jones

Aviation were surprised to see us drive up like that, but they understood the problem and were happy to help us out.

The Airport Authority came in again and said, "You're always finding a way to do things." It sounded like an accusation, as if inventiveness was bad. This time they objected because I couldn't transport fuel over the roads without the proper permit. No matter what we did, the authorities always tried stop us and never lent a helping hand. But I had been able to sell fuel for a while, and I now had the cash to get a full tanker. Fuel sales helped me enormously in selling Huffman Aviation later. I'm extremely grateful to the local aviation industry for rallying behind me in that way.

After I bounced back a bit, I bought a courtesy car. It's normal for a fixed-based operation to have a courtesy car for the captains who fly in. But I needed something extra as an incentive, so I bought a Viper. Every time a captain came in and bought a hundred gallons of fuel oil, he could drive the Viper for an hour at no charge. Sometimes captains bought up to four hundred gallons just so they could have the Viper for the afternoon. They just loved it, and it gave them a great incentive to come to us. To make their visit even better, I created a small putting green for them to use. I tried anything I could to keep the business afloat and my people employed.

Then a new disaster hit—the M&I Bank in Wisconsin called in my loan. When I bought the business, I had put $100,000 down and got a loan with the help of Wally Hilliard as the guarantor. After 9/11, I was not able to always pay on time anymore, and they were sure we were going bankrupt. In addition, creditors were constanly checking my credit due to all the post-9/11 problems and my credit rating had gone down due to the number of inquiries—everytime somebody checked it, I lost five points. I tried to refinance and the only way I got financing was to put my house up as collateral. My previous loan was at three percent, but now the interest was twelve percent. I decided if that was what I had to do, I would do it. I would try to get a better deal in six months when we were back on our feet. At the last moment, that bank withdrew its offer because there was an argument about dirty soil. We had fuel tanks in the ground and the bank said because the ground was contaminated, it couldn't agree to a loan. The contaminated ground had been taken out years before I bought the business, taking care of the problem, but the bank would not listen and refused me a new loan.

One of the other payments I fell behind on was the social security taxes on my employee payroll. On 9/11, I was current, but within six months, I owed the IRS $300,000. The contact person there understood my situation, and asked me what my plan was for repaying the debt.

I told him I'd probably have to sell Huffman Aviation, so he asked me what the company was worth. I told him, "I'm having an appraisal done, and I will give you all the information as it comes in. I understand this must be paid, even though I am not privately responsible." The company was appraised for $3.6 million, even after 9/11. Although we often have such a negative image of the IRS, this gentleman was very pleasant and understanding. I reported to him every month on where things stood and he gave me time to come to a solution. At some point, he was getting a lot of pressure from his boss, asking him where the money from Huffman was. He trusted me and the fact that I was working to resolve the problem so he gave me the space I needed to do so. When I sold the business, I contacted his office and told them they could get their money at the closing, and they got every penny I owed them. I am truly thankful to the IRS for being patient, believing in me, and treating me like decent human being, and I feel it is important to acknowledge what they did for me.

Many people who had nothing to do with the aviation business supported me at that time, as well. People came in off the street to eat in my restaurant. They wanted to see me, shake hands with me, and they made it clear that they understood I was without blame. What they expressed was a lot of gratitude to me for telling the story.

They said, "We are grateful you talked and gave us information when nobody else was willing to tell us the truth. You gave us as much of an explanation as you could, which was all we could ask of you. How could you possibly have known? You're just a businessman; you're not responsible for what your clients do." Because of their support, we survived long enough so that the business didn't go bankrupt, which would have left a lot of unpaid bills and people without jobs.

To my great surprise and disappointment, the Small Business Association refused to help me. I was one of the few companies in our area to suffer big losses because of 9/11. They were prepared to give taxi drivers money because there were fewer clients to drive to and from the airport, but they wouldn't help me. They sent me a letter stating that in the past, I had not paid my bills to the city for the land lease exactly on time, and that was why they didn't want to help.

In the end, I could not get enough help, and I had to sell the business. When I did, I made sure that my employees were taken care of. These people kept their jobs, and most of them still work there. I ended up selling the maintenance business and building to Bob Martin, my director of maintenance. I sold the planes separately and I sold the buildings to Triple Diamond. In the end, the total sale was for about $3.5 million. I paid back the bank, the IRS, and all the outstanding bills. It was heartbreaking to let go of the company, but I feel good about how I managed to close that chapter of my life.

One of the unfortunate things in life is that when you are suddenly in the limelight, even if you did nothing to bring that about, other things start to go wrong, too. People want to take advantage of you because they know that anything associated with you will make them famous. Of course, it happens at the worst possible time, just when you are down and stressed.

After the DOT kicked me out of my own airline and I was not involved in its actual upkeep anymore, I gave Wally Hilliard private advice that I hoped would help him keep the airline alive. I started the company from scratch, knew every part of it, and really cared about it. Around March 2001, he came to me and said that the airline was in desperate need of money and the investors were not willing to put in any more. They felt additional investments needed to be secured because they had already put in so much. Since I owned the building that the airline was housed in, and that building was worth a minimum of $400,000, he asked if I was willing to let him take out a loan using the building as collateral. He promised he would pay the money back in six to eight weeks because he was expecting money from other sources. My relationship with Wally was still good, and I did not think about it twice. I said, "Of course; that's fine."

He made a deal with Kenny Jossett, one of the investors. He would lend the airline $300,000, and I would contribute the building as collateral. Wally put together a document stating that I had borrowed $300,000 from Kenny, and I gave the building as security. According to the terms, I had six months to pay it back.

Then 9/11 happened, and I completely forgot about it, especially since I had not heard anything more about this matter from either Wally or Kenny, though I saw them both on a regular basis. Because of the aviation crisis caused by 9/11, I needed money myself because my own businesses were in trouble. I was not ready to sell Huffman Aviation because I still thought it could be rescued, but I needed an infusion of cash. I decided to sell the building, and found a buyer for $400,000 (the same man who would later buy Huffman Aviation). I went to my closing attorney and said, "Make sure there is no lien on it. I used it to secure a temporary loan a while back." Knowing how casual Wally was about things like that, I thought maybe he had not taken the lien off yet. My attorneys checked and said there was no problem, there was no lien on it, and the closing could go through.

Then I got a call from Wally, and he said, "I need you to wire $300,000 to Kenny."

I answered, "Excuse me?"

"Yes," he said, "You owe him money."

I was incredulous and said, "Wally, that was more than six months ago. You were supposed to pay him back in six to eight weeks. There was no lien on the building, so I assumed you paid Kenny as per our agreement. I never had the money. You borrowed the money; you have to pay it back. I'm not giving you a dime."

Wally said, "If you don't give the money back, it is fraud."

I answered, "I don't know how you see that, Wally. If I never had the money, it's not fraud."

We hung up, and I heard nothing else for a couple of months. Then a detective showed up and very courteously said to me, "Mr. Dekkers, we have a complaint of fraud—money laundering, actually. What is your opinion?"

I said, "Sir, I never received $300,000. Wally Hilliard and the airline were supposed to pay that back, not me. I never knew they hadn't paid it back. Kenny never sent me a letter saying it was not paid, or asked me to give him the building because he was not paid, so I had every reason to assume it was handled."

The detective said, "Yes, I understand that. I guess that makes it a civil case." He left, and again, I heard nothing for a while, until I read on the front page of the newspapers, together with everybody else in my community: "Dekkers Charged with Fraud."

It is an understatement to say that I was surprised. I went to an attorney in Sarasota, and I don't mind admitting that I was nervous.

He asked me very simply, "Did you receive the $300,000?"

I said, "No, I never saw that money. I just signed the papers. I never even read the contract—that is how much I trusted Wally."

He asked me the same question again. "Did you ever receive the money?"

And I told him again, "No, I did not receive the money."

The attorney said, "Well, then the contract you signed was null and void."

My attorney made an agreement with the Assistant District Attorney that if they charged me and needed to arrest me, all they had to do was call him. He would then be in touch with me, and I would report to the police station. Assistant District Attorney David Green said that this would be no problem. After the headlines and the commotion, we heard nothing for weeks. My attorney called every week to see if the judge had signed the arrest warrant, but every time the answer was, "Not yet."

One evening at 6:45 p.m., I was going out for dinner with my wife. I drove out of the development where we lived, and I didn't notice that right outside the gate there were four undercover cars. I drove down the road and they immediately came up behind me with their sirens blaring. They pulled me over and arrested me, right there on the street. Apparently the Collier County sheriff had understood that I should not be arrested at my house. Instead, they had patiently waited for me to drive out.

The arresting officer was a nice guy. He said, "Sir, are you Rudi Dekkers?" I said that I was. He said, "Sir, I don't know why we are arresting you, but you probably know that better than I do."

I said, "I have a feeling I do, but it's different from what we agreed on, because I'm supposed to report myself."

He apologized and said, "I'm sorry because I don't know anything about that, but I have to bring you to the station."

I told him that I understood his position. He apologized for the handcuffs and asked if they were too tight. I told him that it was not comfortable. He said he was sorry again, and then we drove away. I was extremely uncomfortable, physically and emotionally. I had never been arrested and I was very nervous. A nurse took my blood pressure. She asked about my medical history because my blood pressure was 180/120, which is very high. I had never had such high blood pressure before, but I was very tense. It must have been obvious because she asked me several times, "Are you okay?" I told her I was, but that I was diabetic, which she wrote down.

I kept asking, "Do you know what I'm here for? Do you know what I'm charged with?" Nobody would give me an answer. I asked again, and apparently one of the policemen found that obnoxious. He stood in front of me and started yelling, "You goddamn f——ing a——hole, keep your f——ing mouth closed and don't talk to me." The other officers in the hallway later came to me and said, "We know he does that, but it is definitely not approved behavior. If you want to complain, you can, but we already know."

I had too many problems at that time to think of pursuing it, but it was amazingly abusive. They put me in a holding cell, and I had to wait. It was not busy that night, and the whole thing could have been processed in half an hour. The bail was set at $1,000; I was told I had to pay $100 to get out. Because I knew I was going to be charged, I had planned on this and had a great deal of cash in the house. I called my wife and asked her to bring the money. She told me that it wasn't there anymore because she had found it and had used it for groceries. I told her to get some cash somehow and to come and bail me out. At one a.m. in the morning, she finally came, but her delay didn't matter because the sheriff's station took a full four hours to process my papers anyway. The charge was supposed to be a felony but they processed it as a misdemeanor. They let me sit and rot because they were not in a hurry. It must have been obvious that I was not a regular criminal; I was quiet in the holding cell and I didn't give them any trouble, yet they treated me like a criminal.

Of course I made the front page again when I was arrested, and I think that's wrong. The moment you are on the front page, you are considered guilty. For me, it is not just a local matter, this matter was broadcast all over the world. When the judge saw what it was all about, he said, "I can't believe this case. We should not be wasting our time here."

Weeks and weeks dragged on. It was only much later that I understood why all this happened. David Green, who was the Assistant District Attorney in Sarasota, wanted to start his own law office. He needed to get his name known, so he used my media-drawing name to accomplish that. It was no surprise to me to see Green resign as ADA and start his own law firm a short while later.

The new District Attorney didn't want to stop the case because it would make them look bad, so they decided to see if the court would dismiss it. When we went for the arraignments, the District Attorney did not even bother to show up. The judge was not pleased, to say the least. A few weeks later, the District Attorney dropped everything.

Then Wally came to me and said, "You know I'm a guarantor on the loan for Huffman Aviation, so in return, I want some shares." I told him, "I'm sorry, but I won't give them to you. You keep messing up everything. If you're involved with the decision-making process, the company will be destroyed." Bob Martin, my general manager, knew this as well. I had to reassure him that whatever happened, I would make sure Wally would not find himself in that capacity. Wally pressured me for months and threatened that if I did not give him fifty-one percent of the business, he would gather enough votes on the board so he could kick me out of my own company.

He then took me to court to try to prove he was the owner of Huffman Aviation. I came in with a document signed by him a month earlier (something I needed for tax purposes) that said, on Wally's letterhead, with Wally's text, and Wally's signature, that he had no affiliation with Huffman Aviation. The document was faxed to me and the time signature on the document said it had been sent at 4:20 a.m., a time when I am asleep. Wally then claimed I had falsified his signature. He said that I had a key to his office (which I did not), that I broke into his office, and faxed it at four a.m. in the morning.

The judge was angry with Wally and said, "Do you have anything to support those allegations? Do you have a witness? Do you have a handwriting specialist who will confirm that Mr. Dekkers forged your signature?" Of course, they had none of these things. At that point the judge decided the case was closed, and that was the end of that.

I have wondered many times why Wally turned on me, but I think he was just desperate. After 9/11, Florida Air and many other investments fell apart and he panicked. Wally Hilliard was, unfortunately, a very bad businessman in his later years, and I watched him loose $60 million in five years.

Other people, too, wanted to take advantage of me in my vulnerable situation. Vicki Antini was a pretty, young woman in her early twenties. Let me be very clear about this: when I see a young woman the age of one of my daughters, no matter how pretty she is, I am not interested in her. But I understand that customs are different here in America, and it is possible that I might have made comments to her that sounded inappropriate. For instance, one day she came in wearing a beautiful dress, and I told her she looked beautiful that day. The next day, she came in wearing a dress that wasn't ironed, and I said, "You need to iron your clothes; your dress looks terrible when it's all wrinkled." It might have sounded like a personal remark, but it could also have been taken as a comment from an employer to his employee that she was not adhering to my idea of a proper dress code. But I want to make it clear that I never made explicit sexual comments to her and I never touched her.

From the beginning, Vicki had been a problem employee, but I kept shifting her around in the company because I felt sorry for her. I have already told you that she worked as our student coordinator, but she did a terrible job in that position. After I was forced to fire her as student coordinator, I gave her a job in the pilot shop selling merchandise. I received complaints from her supervisor there, as well, and had no choice but to fire her. Before I did, I had a talk with her. I told her that in three different positions, I had my managers tell me that she did not do her work properly. I then gave her two weeks notice. The next day, she stayed out sick, and three days later, I received a letter telling me she was resigning and was going to sue me.

I was not worried about that because I hadn't done anything wrong. I also found out why she was doing this. She had mentioned to one of my employees that she had found a way to get some money so she could go back to college. Apparently, suing me was her way. I hired Paul Murray, an attorney who had helped me with other matters, and we went into mediation.

In the initial stage of the mediation-process, both parties, with their attorneys, meet with the mediator and present their arguments. She was asking for $150,000. I said to my lawyer, "She does not get 150 pennies from me; the only reason she is suing me is to get money to go to college." She said I had been sexually harassing her, and my attorney denied the claim. I was so mad I turned to the mediator and said, "Maybe you could ask if I f——ed her." She immediately replied, "No, he never did that; he never touched me."

In the next part of the mediation process, the parties sit in separate offices and the mediator goes back and forth between the two rooms relaying the proposed compromises. From $150,000, she went down to a $100,000. My answer to her was that I hadn't done anything, and she wouldn't get $500. The next offer was $50,000. It went down quickly, and when they came back with an offer of $25,000, my attorney counseled me to take it. I refused. He said, "You need to take it; it's a lot more expensive if you fight it." I refused. The mediator came back with an offer of $15,000.

My attorney said, "Rudi, if you don't do this right now, I'm resigning as your attorney and you can do it all yourself because this is less than the bill that you'll receive from me." I said no way.

The mediator asked, "What are you willing to pay?"

I answered, "I'm not willing to pay anything."

My attorney said, "Rudi, please offer them $10,000. If you don't, I will walk out of here." I had used Paul for many other business deals, so I gave in because I could see that he meant it, and I did not want him to be mad at me. So she got her ten grand, with the understanding that the case was sealed. Huffman Aviation was struggling, and I did not have $10,000, so we agreed that I would make two $5,000 payments. I paid the first installment on time, but the second one was a few days late. At that point, she went to the news and talked about the case, feeling she no longer had to abide by her side of the agreement. But I kept my end of the bargain and she was paid.

I SURVIVE

I am ready to die, so I do not panic, though my lungs are full of ice cold water, and I am hanging in my seatbelt, upside down, in my crashed helicopter at the bottom of the Caloosahatchee River.

Then, a thought of my granddaughter Brooke flashes through me. She's a very special little girl to me, although there are not many people who know that. She was born exactly one year after September twelfth. When she was born and I went to the hospital to see her, I had a feeling of love so overwhelming that I can't begin to describe it. She is the light in my life. When I think of her, I know I really do want to live. I want to get out of there and see her grow up.

A voice in my head says, "Calm down; you will not survive if you panic." In a moment, I suddenly know the solution to the seatbelt problem. I take off my leather jacket one arm at a time, and in a few seconds I am free of my shoulder harness. I still feel no shortage of air, but I have no time to wonder about that. They later calculated that I was underwater for thirteen or fourteen seconds, but in stressful situations, your body handles things in unusual ways.

I don't want to swim out through the windshield because it's broken and I am afraid there might be sharp splinters sticking out that will rip me to shreds. Nor do I want to go out the opposite door, which is pointing up, because I am afraid I will loose my sense of direction if I leave my seat.

With my foot, I find a small space between the door and the sandy bottom of the river. Because the skid is wider than the helicopter, it is on a slight angle. I put my leg between the door and the sand, and I push the helicopter up with my leg. I don't know where I got the strength from at that moment. I feel the helicopter come up a little bit, and I slide out. The only damage I realized later from that accident is the skin I lost on my shinbone where I lifted the helicopter up. It took a long time to heal, and I still have the scar.

I float to the surface of the water. For the first time, I realize that I am very, very cold. One of the skids is sticking out of the shallow water, and I hold on to it, coughing and throwing up water. It takes me fifteen seconds to recoup, and I try to think of what to do next while I still have my strength. I am exhausted, and I calculate that the shore is maybe three hundred yards away. The current runs east to west, and I have to swim to the south; I know I will never make it, even though I am a strong swimmer. I have to get out of the water because it is about 50 degrees, and I will have hypothermia in just a couple of minutes.

Hanging on to the skid makes me so cold that I slide back further into the water, knowing its relative warmth will give me a couple of seconds of extra energy. For a few moments, I don't know what to do. I just hang on to the skids with my arms folded in such a way that if I pass out, I will still hang there (something I learned in the military during survival training). I figure that eventually, somebody will find me and bring me to the hospital.

Suddenly, I hear a helicopter approaching. It is Tony, who has flown back to look for me. I can tell that he has seen my helicopter in the water and has found me hanging on the skid. I wave to him and he lowers his helicopter above me. I am confused and try to figure out what the hell he is doing. Then I remember that he flew helicopters during the Gulf War and knows how to rescue people. He comes down far enough so I can put my arm around one of his skids. I put my arms in a lock on his skid, thinking again that if I pass out, I will still hang on to his helicopter.

He flies me to shore, to the south side of the river. He hovers five to six feet above somebody's lawn and I let myself fall. Though it is just a few feet, it is extremely painful because I am so unbelievably cold, and for a moment, I think I've broken both my legs. I stay down for at least five seconds without moving. Then I hear the helicopter above me and I realize I have to show Tony that I am okay, so I wave at him. He flies off, since there is no place for him to land right there.

Now that I am in the open air, the cold is unbearable. The house whose lawn I have fallen on has a pool, and I think the water must be warmer than the air, so I jump into the pool. I am sure there is nobody at home, but I found out later that people in the house saw me going into their pool and didn't do anything to stop me or help me. The warmth of the water in the pool gives me a bit more strength, but I can't stay there. I have to get to the street and find somebody to take me to a hospital. I walk into the street and see a man walking to his car. I walk up to the guy and say to him, with chattering teeth, "I crashed my helicopter into the river. Can you please bring me to the hospital?"

The guy looks at me and drives away. Somebody else sees this incident, walks up to me, and says, "I live close by. Come with me and I'll bring you to the hospital." I can barely walk, but by the time I have walked about a hundred yards with him, an ambulance drives up.

The EMT asks for my name, and then asks what has happened. In the meantime, they peel me out of my wet clothes. There is one male nurse and two female nurses, so the male nurse says, "Can you hold this blanket so the nurses won't see you when I undress you?"

I make a joke then. Looking down into my pants, I say, "Do you really think there is something there to see?"

They laugh, and he says, "You really don't care?"

I answer, "I assume they've seen it all before, but maybe I should get their phone numbers and talk to them later."

They put a silver foil suit on me and tell me I am fifteen degrees under-cooled, close to going into shock. They are surprised I am still clear-headed and able to make tasteless jokes. The only thing I know is that I am unbelievably tired. They drive me the short distance to the Lee Memorial Hospital emergency room, where they process me immediately. They put me on an intravenous line with warm fluid, and it feels strange to have the hot liquid going up into my arm. About an hour later, I am feeling pretty good.

I make the mistake of not telling anybody close to me what has happened. I do not think it is a good idea to call my wife or my friends. I think I'll just tell them all about it later, when I am home again and everything is fine. What I do not realize is that when anything happens to me, it is instant news. While I am trying to protect them from the scary news, the news stations have already blasted "Rudi Dekkers, owner of Huffman Aviation, in helicopter crash," all over God's creation. At 7:30 a.m., the world has already heard about my latest adventure. Everybody who knows me is in a panic, wondering what has happened to me. Not until this accident do I realize that I am a kind of public figure and that this will stay with me all my life.

Meanwhile, I am still concerned about signing over Huffman Aviation that day. As far as I am concerned, if there is any way I can make it happen, the sale will go through. My doctor is very blunt and says, "You're not going anywhere." But a few hours later, the x-rays have confirmed that nothing has been broken, and around 11:30 am, I tell him again, "I really need to get to an important business meeting."

By complete coincidence, my doctor is a helicopter pilot too. He keeps saying, "Man, oh, man, you were so lucky. There are usually no survivors after a helicopter crashes in the water." I tell him, "It's not just luck, it's also my training." I know that if I had not had that special training from John, I would have died that morning. Finally, the doctor gives me the go-ahead and tells me to sign the release form and to dress myself. I stand up and I collapse immediately. I am still much too weak. The doctor smiles at me and says, "I guess you're not going quite yet, are you?"

I stay another two hours, and at two p.m., I feel strong enough to leave. Wally Hilliard picks me up from the hospital and drives me to Ft. Myers, where he has his plane. It is eerie to be at the same airport I had left that morning. We fly to Venice in his airplane, but I do not completely trust Wally's ability as a pilot, so I watch him like a hawk the whole way. We fly over the exact spot where I crashed that morning, and I see my helicopter in the water. That really frightens me. It took me a long time before I could approach that spot without fear.

We arrive in Venice and everybody thinks it is great that I've made it. I go into the meeting, and at six p.m., we sign the documents finalizing the sale. I go home, and the reporters are waiting for me there. They ask me if I can go to the Naples news station with them and give them an interview. I decide I might as well get it over with. It isn't until after that interview that I can actually go home.

I have not communicated to my wife that I am all right, so when I get home, she is pretty angry. I did not understand it then, but looking at it from her point of view, I do now. But I am a very strong person, and the next morning at nine a.m., I am playing tennis again.

A combination of luck in having Tony there to get me out of the water before hypothermia set in, and the training I got from John allowed me survive. That, and not panicking, even when everything looked hopeless, because when you panic, you cannot act in your own best interest. That is how you kill yourself.

The FAA looks over my helicopter after it is taken out of the water (the NTSB only investigates when an aviation accident results in death). Initially, I am not allowed to personally see and inspect the helicopter. After their investigation, they tell me they had checked everything, and there was simply no fuel in the tank. They rule that the accident was due to pilot error and are getting ready to pull my license.

When I get the helicopter back after their investigation, I see that they have done a very superficial job. Normally, the FAA or NTSB don't bother putting the pieces back together after a thorough investigation. In the past, sometimes all I have gotten back were piles of airplane parts. In this case, the helicopter is returned to me looking exactly as it had when it came out of the water. They determined that there was no fuel in the tank and assumed pilot error. They never looked further and failed to check if the fuel lines were tight.

I knew beyond the shadow of any doubt that there had been fuel in the tank when I did my preflight check, so I check the helicopter out. The evidence I find is chilling. Two screws that clamp the fuel lines are loose; the safety wire is still on, but the wires themselves have been cut. A safety wire is a wire threaded through the nut and tied to the frame of the helicopter somewhere. Even if the nut comes loose, it cannot turn, which is important because there is so much vibration in a helicopter that things come loose rather easily.

I am convinced it had never been checked by the FAA mechanic because when they check the screws, they cut the safety wire off and remove it. Only then do they unscrew the screws. But this wire has been cut and put back, to make it look as if everything was okay. On the preflight check, it would appear fine, but there is absolutely no doubt about it: the screws had been loosened and this had clearly caused the crash. When a helicopter is flying, the gas tank becomes pressurized and there is pressure in the fuel lines. With the screws loose, the fuel would be fine as long as the helicopter was sitting still. But it would spurt out the moment you started flying. You would have only a few minutes of flying time before all the fuel was lost.

I call my contact at the FAA and say, "Tell me again about my empty tank."

He replies, "Rudi, you have to believe me. There was no fuel, I mean, not a single drop! There is no doubt about it, Rudi; you made a mistake with your fuel. It was your own fault, and the FAA will definitely pull your license." They were really convinced it had been my fault for not checking the fuel before takeoff.

I then call the Hiller Helicopter factory and ask George, the owner, to talk to me about the fuel situation. He tells me that even when you run out of fuel, there would still be fuel left—the so-called "unusable fuel." In my helicopter, that would have been 2.5 gallons. I am elated and say, "Thanks, man, you just saved my license!"

I call the FAA back and say, "Tell me how much unusable fuel is in that particular tank when it's empty."

There is silence on the phone line. He finally says, "Let me look up the specs for that model." He comes back and acknowledges that there should have been 2.5 gallons of fuel left in the tank when it was on "empty." If it really had been my fault, the tank would not have been completely empty; there would have been 2.5 gallons left. Since there was nothing left, that could only be true if it had sprayed out under pressure.

Somebody deliberately tampered with my helicopter. It was an attempt on my life. If I had drowned in the river, it would have looked like an accident. It would have been blamed on pilot error; nobody would have thought to look at anything else once they discovered the empty tank. They would have assumed that I had not done my preflight check correctly. There may have been pilots who knew me well and who would have raised their eyebrows at that conclusion. They would know how consistent and careful I always am in my preflight checks, but they would have had no choice but to concur. In case of death, the NTSB would have performed the investigation and maybe they would have uncovered the evidence, as I did. I can only hope.

The crash happened just hours before I was going to sell Huffman Aviation. I have no idea if this was a coincidence or not. I was selling it because I was cash poor, and I wanted my employees to have a boss who could guarantee them their salaries. If I hadn't sold, I would have gone bankrupt. I can't think of anybody who would have benefited from the bankruptcy, so it is hard to imagine who would have sabotaged my helicopter. I assume that one of the people who made death threats when I said I didn't want any more Muslim students made good on their threats. Perhaps an unstable person thought I was responsible for 9/11 and wanted me dead. I still have no idea.

I had a dilemma on my hands. I could go to the police with the evidence and ask them to investigate the attempt on my life. I could tell them that I left the helicopter the night before in good shape and that the flight the day before had been uneventful. Sometime during the night, somebody with access to that location had tampered with my helicopter. Since it was a brief window of time and a small area, there would be only a limited number of people who could have done it. However, I knew going to the police would mean newspaper headlines and all the fuss that went with it. And I had more pressing reason to be concerned about publicity.

After 9/11 and the collapse of my companies, I had started a new venture, a fractional company called Florida Air Share. Fractional companies allow a number of people to buy a plane together. They agree to share the costs of the purchase and maintenance, and each person gets a certain number of hours flying time. I came up with the idea of doing a fractional lease where you lease a portion of the plane for a portion of the flying time. When you buy the plane outright, as with traditional fractionals, you have a huge cost up front (the way you do if you were to buy a car without financing); with a lease, the cost is spread out over time. The company was young, and I had high hopes for it.

I was afraid that if people thought somebody was tampering with my planes, I would lose the people who had shown an interest in Florida Air Share. I did not get my helicopter back until months after the attempt, anyway, and I figured that any evidence that could have been gathered right after it happened would have been destroyed by now. I decided to let the matter rest, rather than go to the police and have this investigation destroy my new company.

MY STORY CONTINUES

As it turned out, my willingness to let the person who tried to murder me walk away was not enough to make my new plans prosper. The new FAA fractional law was not yet in effect when I started Florida Air Share. When the FAA asked what I was doing, they determined that I was doing it legally. I am very careful with the law, and my lawyers and I had made sure that everything was above board. It was agreed that my company was grandfathered in for the time being; I was waiting for the new laws to come out, and then we would make sure to comply with what the FAA would want.

One woman at the FAA took a dislike to me and insisted I was doing illegal charters. No matter how clear it was that I was not breaking any laws, she decided I was going to be shut down. She argued that a lease did not constitute ownership. However, by their own rules and regulations, it showed that if you have a multiple-year lease, it is considered the same as ownership. But they were threatening me with a $200,000 fine, so it looked like I had no choice, especially since I didn't have the money to sue them. They insisted that part of the deal was that I would never have a commercial charter company again, further hampering my ability to make a living. All I could do was make sure all my customers were taken care of and close down this company, as I had done with my previous companies.

The combinations of all these stresses and setbacks took a devastating toll on my personal life. My marriage to Astrid had not been ideal, but I think it would not have fallen apart if it hadn't been for the stress all these troubles caused us. My divorce from Astrid, after twenty years of marriage, was a personal and painful episode.

Back in March of 2002, I started to feel physically terrible. I had to pee at night, and I was drinking a lot of water. It happened very gradually, and because of the huge business and personal problems in my life I wasn't paying too much attention to it initially. Eventually I went to the doctor and she ordered a battery of tests. When I came back to hear the results of the test, she told me I had a problem with high blood sugar. At that time, I did not even know exactly what that meant, but my blood sugar count was 380. I also weighed 250 pounds, and since I'm six foot tall that was at least sixty pounds overweight. My doctor told me I had to lose weight and reduce my stress level or else I wouldn't see my sixtieth birthday. She knew what I was going through and that my stress levels were through the roof.

The problem with diabetes is that initially, you don't feel bad, and that makes it difficult to take the symptoms seriously. But I knew my doctor was serious and I had to make some changes. I started cutting down on refined carbohydrates, and I have gradually lost sixty pounds over the course of two years. We have discovered that I am actually insulin resistant, which adds another level of complication. The lowest my blood sugar normally goes is about 180. If I go too long without eating, I get dizzy and it goes to 120. In my case, it is definitely stress that is causing diabetes. I've been told that this disease cannot be "fixed," and I will have to live with this until I die, and I will always have to obey certain dietary rules. I have managed, as have thousands of other diabetics, to find a way to live with this disease.

Life after 9/11 has changed for many of the people in my life, too. I went to the Venice Airport recently and it was very quiet compared to the busy and lively times before 9/11. The contrast was almost spooky. Talking with people there, I found out that the flight school business was down to about twenty percent of what it used to be. Nationally, flight schools are doing about sixty percent of the business they used to do. There is beginning to be a shortage of pilots in the US. Though no law has been passed about this, there is now an informal understanding in this country that to be a commercial pilot, you need to be a citizen. This is starting to create a shortage which will get bigger as time goes on, and it will be interesting to see how that resolves itself.

After losing almost everything I had, I am rebuilding a good life for myself. To my great joy, I am now married to Katia, a wonderful woman of Cuban descent who is an American citizen. We are the very happy and proud parents of a beautiful baby girl, Angeline

Bianca Chantal Dekkers, who was born on October 8, 2008, and fills my days with joy.

I remain an optimist. I still love this country for what it stands for. I still love the American people, and I still believe in the American dream. I believe that I will rebuild a good life for myself and that some good will come out of this mess.

EPILOGUE

As this book was going to print, the world discovered that history's most sought after terrorist, Osama bin Laden , was finally dead. Surprisingly, he was found living in Abbottabad, Pakistan not on a rugged mountainside.

Once again we are reminded of all those who were victimized by the events of 9/11, and their painful losses. However, as the highly emotional, spontaneous gathering at Ground Zero made clear, the death of bin Laden is an important piece of closure.

Terrorists, men and women who strike out and kill innocent people, are of all nationalities and religions. They are the enemy of ordinary people. Hopefully, this event will lessen the bitterness which has led to hostility against patriotic, good citizens in this country who happen to be Muslim.

It was my intention in telling my story, that the difference between the implied guilt and true innocence becomes somewhat clearer. In dire circumstances, many rush to judgment because of fear or anger. However, pointing a finger at a random person who has skin color or religion in common with terrorists, or blaming a person who did business with people who much later turn out to be terrorists, can in no way contribute to making this a safer country. It is up to all of us to hold ourselves to a higher standard, and to judge each man and woman by the "contents of their character" as Martin Luther King so eloquently said.

It has taken ten difficult years to get to this point, and still men and women, of various countries, are still at war on foreign soil in the aftermath of 9/11. It is my profound hope that we can go forward with courage and confidence to build a world in which terrorism is made impossible simply because we choose to recognize our commonality. We can decide to leave our children a world filled with peace.